21218
√94

MIND YOUR OWN BUSINESS

NORMAN JASPAN

PRENTICE-HALL, INC.
Englewood Cliffs, N.J.

Library of Congress Cataloging in Publication Data

Jaspan, Norman.
      Mind your own business.

      1.   Employee theft—United States.   2.   Retail trade—
Security measures.   I.   Title.
HF5387.J35   658.4'7   74–6417
ISBN 0-13-583427-9

This book is dedicated to my father
ISAAC A. JASPAN
who proved by example that integrity
need be no hindrance to
success in business

ACKNOWLEDGMENTS

I would like to express my indebtedness to Nicholas O. Prounis and Elizabeth V. Long, whose command of the problem, advice, and unflagging patience have meant so much to me in the shaping of the book. I also want to thank Walter Nagel, Jay McCracken, and the other members of the staff of Norman Jaspan Associates for their help and invaluable suggestions. Finally I wish to express my gratitude and love to my wife Jeanne and my children Michael David and Ronald Howard for their forbearance.

PREFACE

There are a thousand hacking at the branches of
evil to one who is striking at the root . . .
                                        Henry David Thoreau

Over the past forty years, we have watched the trend of white collar crime accelerate. Fifteen years ago, in *The Thief in the White Collar,* we identified employee dishonesty as beginning to have a pervasive influence in the business world because of mergers, acquisitions, decentralization of operations, computerization, and the displacement of owner-managers.

In the intervening years, industry and government have mounted a huge effort against crime in business with little to show for it except the proliferation of uniformed guards, saturation by TV cameras and other electronic devices, and the widespread use of lie detector tests—all at great cost to the economy and in human relations. Business losses due to dishonesty are at an all-time high.

Theft is odious and contemptible, but you can't run a business on fear. An organization can be destroyed overnight by an overreaction to the discovery of theft—lashing out furiously at everybody, the good and the bad. But an organization can also literally be destroyed by employee theft, and if not destroyed, demoralized and depleted.

What is clearly needed is an approach that is humane with a sense of proportion and professionalism. The problem can best be dealt with by businesslike procedures and policies that are fair, just, and easily enforceable.

For nearly a half century, Norman Jaspan Associates and its affiliates have been providing top management, internationally, with vital facts concerning the causes of inventory losses, manipulations, conflicts of interest, kickbacks, and other employee malpractices.

Equally important, its engineers design measures for the long-term protection of company assets, tangible and intan-

v

gible, by establishing practical controls, and conduct educational programs that revitalize and motivate employees.

The malpractices that receive the least attention are those committed by the employee who holds a position of trust, whose opportunity is great, whose method is less subject to question—and frequently the last to be suspected. The product of a good college education, he has been exposed to all the cultural values that Western civilization holds dear. Yet, he has become America's most resourceful and successful thief.

It is too easy to attribute escalating losses to a general decline in moral standards. People are basically honest when they come to work for you—all too often the workplace becomes the school for dishonesty.

This book reveals why very few business crimes see the light of day in court. Management must, therefore, as President Truman so aptly put it, realize that "The buck stops here."

Responsibility for the integrity of a company and its employees begins and ends with the chief executive, and he cannot delegate his stewardship to subordinates who might be most at fault. There is no other segment of the American economy that can play a greater role in setting the moral tone in which business is conducted.

Attention is also directed to how business methods—profit sharing, incentive programs, mergers, stock options —intended to be positive factors can corrupt honest employees. It also reveals how dishonesty which often stems from permissiveness, neglect and opportunity—and all too frequently from the influence of unrealistic management pressures—constitutes a drain on profits, inflates the price of goods and services for the consumer, and may ultimately destroy the foundation of our society.

Since no purpose would be served by identifying the individuals and firms involved, the names and locations in the cases cited have been changed or omitted.

The case histories are presented in order to assist management—by taking it behind the scenes to visualize what went wrong, by showing what corrective measures were taken and indicating how these principles can be applied by every one whose primary concern is how best to *Mind Your Own Business*.

NORMAN JASPAN

CONTENTS

I	True Confessions—Business Edition	1
II	Hung by the Old School Tie	13
III	Intelligence, Yes; Magic, No!	23
IV	Those Gullible Conglomerates	41
V	Why They Bite the Hand That Feeds them	61
VI	School for Dishonesty	81
VII	How Pressure for Results Creates Opportunists	93
VIII	Reverse Incentives in Merchandising	105
IX	Kickbacks: A $5-Billion Ripoff	115
X	Figures That Lie	139
XI	How to Guard Trade Secrets	153
XII	Sick Hospitals	169
XIII	Castles or Prisons?	185
XIV	Security You Can Afford	189
	Summary—Questions and Answers	201

1 TRUE CONFESSIONS—
BUSINESS EDITION

The best way to bring home the full extent of business crime is to cite some examples from among the hundreds of confessions in our files. This one was excerpted from a typical statement made by a trusted employee of a nationally known department store.

. . . I am thirty-eight years old, married, and have two children. My wife is a Sunday School teacher and is active in community affairs. I just bought a new Pontiac which is being financed through GMAC. Three years ago I purchased a $31,500 split-level home on which I pay $176 per month. My wife and I have a joint account with a balance of about $1,700. I have been employed here for eleven years and presently work in the shipping department. My earnings are $192 per week.

. . . I admit that I have been stealing from the store for at least six years. Some of the merchandise I kept for myself, and some I sold. I also shipped out items as gifts for my family and friends. It was easy to do, and it made me feel important.

. . . Several other store employees helped me to steal, and in turn I helped them. This includes my supervisor and other department heads. A few of the most recent stolen items that are still in my home are a 25-horsepower outboard motor, a portable TV set, two Polaroid cameras, a Winchester rifle, a hi-fi set, and two transistor radios. I also stole customer returns, including toys, tools, outdoor grills, folding chairs, etc., which I believe are still in my basement.

. . . The following are some of the ways that I stole:

1. I had access to pads of address labels and used them to send goods to myself, my friends, and members of my family.

2. The supervisors never really bothered to read what they were signing, so that it was no problem to get my package passes approved. I was also able to reuse passes that the exit guard failed to pick up.

3. I did the same thing with old sales slips that were never collected, reusing them as well.

4. I obtained merchandise by falsely claiming the orders I received to pack for shipment were short. I would then get extra goods and mail them to my family or friends.

5. From time to time I would short-ship customers, keep the merchandise, and get it out of the store in one of the ways mentioned above.

6. I would buy damaged merchandise at a very low price and substitute good items in its place before taking it home.

7. I would have my wife or a friend return stolen merchandise for a cash refund.

8. I would telephone the store, order any merchandise I wanted, and have it sent C.O.D. to a wrong address. I knew the item would eventually come back to me, and I could take it home. The system was such that the department that made the sale would never know that they did not get their goods back.

. . . There were many other ways to obtain the things I wanted, but the easiest was by working with Harvey Collins in the returns room. Harvey would get me items from customer returns, after putting through the necessary credit slips. The selling departments didn't check their returns, so they didn't realize that the goods weren't being sent back to their stockrooms.

. . . In the last year alone I would estimate that my thefts amounted to at least $15,000, maybe more. It's impossible for me to guess what the total figure adds up to over the past six years, although I know that my stealing increased considerably after I bought my home. . . .

In this case, the employee and others implicated by him, who also signed acknowledgments of their thefts, were discharged. They were not arrested, nor were they compelled to make restitution. The firing of dishonest employees, unfortunately, does little to solve the underlying problem of internal theft.

When dishonesty comes to light, the initial management reaction is characteristically one of dismay. Executives are disturbed to learn that such a thing has happened—that it could happen—in their company. During the initial period of shock, serious soul-searching takes place, and perhaps some high-level conferences. Then gradually the effect wears off and, with the vague hope that the situation is under control, business as usual is resumed.

We have seen buyers, supervisors, and even top-level executives separated from their jobs in a single, sweeping housecleaning. But in many instances the underlying conditions are not affected in the slightest degree.

Significantly, employees are basically honest when they start to work for you—they are like your daughter and my son, with all the benefits of a good home environment and education. Then, unfortunately, they are exposed to the school for dishonesty, the workplace. Employees are influenced by the good or bad examples of their supervisors.

Dishonesty in a company is frequently a barometer of the quality and integrity of supervision. A half dozen honest supervisors who really do their jobs can keep a hundred employees honest, while a couple who are dishonest, disinterested, or disloyal will result in a hundred dishonest employees. It takes a lifetime to build an organization, and there is no gratification in catching dishonest employees. Therefore, it is incumbent on management to make every effort to keep honest people honest.

Our firm uncovered more than $100 million worth of employee dishonesty in the last year. Supervisors were responsible for 62 percent of it. This is not to say that rank-and-file dishonesty is insignificant, but the big dollar losses by far are due to middle management and executive personnel.

It is easier to sit behind a desk and manipulate, take kickbacks, and pass out confidential information than to back up a truck once a week and steal merchandise. The following excerpt from a confession is all too-typical:

> I am a Ph.D. and have been employed for about nine years as Director, Physical Research Labs. I realize I was dishonest.
>
> . . . I took formulas, slides, chemical tests, blueprints, and other records which are the sole property of this company.
>
> . . . I took studies of biological activity, compounds, and other confidential records which I shipped to a professor on the West Coast. The contents were marked "Reprints—Educational Material." This information, together with the results of research undertaken by the professor under

grants made to his university, was to be the basis of a joint venture in conflict with my current employer.

There is no telling how many people are seriously affected, even destroyed by being caught in white-collar crime, but the number is very high. The general public does not see even the tip of the iceberg. Only 5 percent of these crimes end up before the courts, and approximately 1 percent of those involved receive a sentence of a year or more.

The first principle on which we work: *The great majority of people are basically honest and decent.*

Then what happens? Why do so many basically honest and decent people become dishonest on the job? Here are the words of a confessed thief—a divisional manager:

> Headquarters was pressuring me for a net of at least 5 percent per quarter. In the spring it was plain to me that we would not achieve this. It was a temporary situation which would work itself out, but the second quarter would be bad. Mr. Thorson took me aside and said: "What are you getting all worked up for? All they do is look at your performance figures. The people who take the inventory are just clerks. Let me show you how you can get around this situation and maybe you can do me a good turn sometime." When he showed me I saw how easy it was. . . .

The second principle: *Our businesses and institutions often become schools for dishonesty—by pressure, by example, by temptation, but most of all by poor management.*

> I am the supervisor of the mailroom and courier service. I have done a lot of dishonest things in the past three years. I used and sold other people's

credit cards which I obtained when I opened the mail. I tore up company records, customer charges, and complaints hoping to avoid suspicion. I duplicated newly approved account lists and sold them for a dollar a name. I averaged about a thousand names a month. This was going on before I came here.

Another principle: *The first indication of dishonesty in an enterprise will lead, if followed skillfully, to other defalcations.*

Uncovering a quarter of a million dollar defalcation is routine; uncovering even a million dollar defalcation is not unusual. Here are a few examples from our files.

Credit Department: I have been controller here for eleven years. Accounts receivable including credit and collection are also my responsibilities.

Once each month all of the accounts for credit customers are examined for past due indebtedness for aging. I had a competent man working under me as credit manager. I was planning to recommend him for controller since I anticipated a promotion to an executive position, when I discovered that he was playing around with the aging of accounts.

He was disguising the true delinquent status of accounts, which I presumed was done to stay within allowable limits. To my regret, I have now been informed that it was done to obviate investigating many defalcations. He was in collusion with store salesmen and his collection staff. The salesmen were paid commissions at the time of sale. Many sales turned out to be bad risks and, in some cases, fictitious orders. The repossessed merchandise was bought back at a fraction of its value and disposed of to their own customers, such as landlords who provide furnished apartments.

I felt that if the manipulations of aging of accounts became known to top management, it would be a reflection on me. In order to protect myself, I had to bury approximately $750,000 worth of misstated write-offs to final resting places without anyone knowing about it.

International Department: As manager of the Export Department I admit that I have taken advantage of my position for at least ten years. I became involved in kickbacks, falsification of figures, conflicts of interest, collusion with purchasing agents, reps, and others. It accelerated when I discovered that instead of being promoted I had a new boss. We never got along, and I felt he would fire me at the first opportunity.

So I started to make my connections because I felt I would have to go into business for myself. I set up dummy sales agencies, companies, and corporations in collusion with our sales reps, in order to siphon off excessive commissions. My businesses grew fantastically as a result of these connections, and I was making between $50,000 and $100,000 per year until this day.

These arrangements are a way of life with many of my associates and counterparts in other companies throughout the world.

Sales Department: I'm employed as district sales manager of the heavy machinery manufacturing division. I am with this company thirty-one years, and am retiring at the end of this month with a pension of $730 a month. The company has already presented me with the keys to a $5,000 car as a farewell gift. My salary is $22,000 a year plus an override and some other incentives.

I never earned more than $30,000 a year on this job. This barely covered my income tax, as my income from my other activities was in excess of $65,000 a year.

This company sells only new machinery. The

business that I set up was the acquisition and sale of *used* machinery. I sold to many of the contacts that I developed as an employee here, feeling they would eventually be customers for new equipment. I still believe my philosophy was right to this day. I sold new equipment, as a rule, by first selling used equipment from my own company.

I used my employer's technicians and estimators (most of whom were working on private jobs for me and independently for themselves around the country on company time and expense) and replacement parts to further my own business at the expense of my employer.

Purchasing Department: My responsibilities as manager of capital purchasing include assisting in setting up policy, managing the contractors we engage, plant purchasing, and stores operations. I have two construction purchasing agents, a buyer, three storekeepers and a secretary working for me. Some of the ways in which I took advantage of my position are as follows:

I allowed favored vendors to obtain business at prices higher than the market called for.

I awarded bids to favored vendors after advising them and guiding them as to other bids submitted.

I discouraged bona fide vendors with my deliberate procrastinations and by giving them misleading and incomplete information.

I received 20 percent of the fee on rented equipment.

I have calculated that if I had done my job honestly, total purchases and overall costs could have been reduced a minimum of 12 percent.

The real fruits of investigation lie in what is learned. Information must be used intelligently to explain to management its implications and the corrective measures that are necessary to enable the enterprise to be well run and profitable—and, I might add, to give basically decent people the opportunity to work without being exposed to a corrupting atmosphere.

At Norman Jaspan Associates we uncover the essential facts—and then act on them. But as we all know, the truth, particularly about conspiracy to commit illegal acts, is often hard to discover. Some companies try to get at it through lie detector tests and electronic surveillance equipment. That is not the way to do it. We get at the truth in a simpler way. We talk to people. And when we talk with them, we bring to bear a combination of three things: sound principles of behavioral science; general knowledge of how people act and react in organizations; and specific knowledge and in-depth understanding of the particular industry or function that is under study.

We are successful because our approach embodies these essential principles. The knack lies in applying the principles ethically, humanely, and compassionately with a sense of proportion that is sensitive to the rights and dignity of people and to the vital importance of preserving morale in an organization.

We have other things going for us when we approach an interview. We have done our homework and know a great deal already (although we never disclose how much we know). Even more important, we know certain things about people. We know that many employees, including department heads, supervisors, and executives, are aware of malpractices but do nothing about them in order to avoid a distasteful situation. This is not to say that these executives are permissive or condone misdeeds. They simply emotionally withdraw from a situation that may involve friends or associates; or they do not want to disturb the even tenor of their own departments; or they are afraid of being found at fault themselves and criticized; or they may be intimidated by fear of bodily harm or loss of job. Nevertheless, guilty knowledge is a burden. When we approach people in the correct way, they will take the opportunity to get rid of the burden . . . but only if they are not challenged directly to do so.

There is a big difference between an *interview* and an *interrogation*. An interview is a fact-finding effort —questions and answers about subjects, frequently quite bland, that are not threatening. An interrogation is a much more penetrating procedure. For us, a cardinal point in getting at the truth is to keep the discussion on the "interview" level as long as possible. If interrogation seems justified, then the transition should be led into so gradually that the employee does not immediately realize what is happening. In the best-run interview, he may never realize it.

Two factors are at work here. For one thing, the employee, while not exactly off his guard, is reasonably at ease. The conversation has been relaxed, and he sees no reason not to make other small disclosures when the questions are asked. By themselves, small disclosures do not indicate anything adverse to him. Given the smooth, cordial way in which the interview is progressing, he feels there is no reason to withhold information on a particular subject.

Thus a simple interview can accomplish a great deal. The interviewer builds up an authoritative picture of the organization under study, with particular emphasis on what is wrong. The employee discloses facts that he didn't even know he possessed.

Now the conversation eases into more "sensitive" areas. If he has knowledge that will be helpful, he is going to tell us about it. If he is involved in something dishonest, he will have every opportunity to unburden himself.

At this point in the interview we may have gotten about all we can get from a person not personally involved in illicit activities, but who may know that such activities exist. But maybe the employee is not just an innocent observer. Here is where a skilled interviewer can bring out more of the truth. Often he hears more than he had reason to expect.

The skilled interviewer needs only a minimum of evidence surrounding a loss to estimate fairly accurately the extent of the loss as well as to reconstruct the events that preceded it. Uncovering the extent of the theft and the persons involved requires perceptiveness and unusual skills in interviewing.

The actual confrontation is a critical point in the interviewing process. It is important at this time to make it a meeting of two persons seeking a resolution to a problem, rather than of two adversaries.

Clients are usually astonished when they see suspects become meek, penitent, and ready to tell all. One observer, the medical director of one of New York's largest and most prestigious hospitals, who was present at some key interviews, later told members of the board:

> It was shocking and painful to see fine, professional men—the heads of purchasing, pharmacy, accounting, and others come in, blurt out their misdeeds and all but beat their breast before me. Later, when I thought about it as a physician, I saw that psychologically it makes sense. A man begins with a little chiseling, and inch by inch works his way up to a pattern of living which he enjoys but which rests on a morally loathsome basis. Then Jaspan probes the sore, and suddenly the man wants to get rid of the stored-up guilt all at once. The interrogation seems to offer him a cheap, easy way to pay off. Jaspan is really an expert practicing psychologist without knowing it.

Finally the employee has told the interviewer everything, and he is more relaxed than he may have been for months or perhaps even years. He is free of what has been gnawing at him. We are now at a pivotal point in the conduct of a typical case. Obviously it is not where the case begins. And it is not where the case ends.

We are now in a position to deal with reality, rather than simply with a textbook solution to a business problem. We have identified supervisory shortcomings, procedural deficiencies, physical flaws, and poor performance that adversely affect profits. The formulation of corrective measures which are practical, easily enforceable, and tailored to your individual needs can be expeditiously introduced.

2 HUNG BY THE OLD
SCHOOL TIE

Quite rightfully, citizens everywhere are aroused and fearful over crime in the streets. But does the average businessman know (or is he willing to admit) that street crime runs a very poor second place, both in dollars and cents lost and in the number of participants, to business thefts? Employee dishonesty rarely makes the headlines. Relatively few arrests are made; fewer cases are tried. Nevertheless, for the businessman it is this latter problem that should present the greater concern.

The largest percentage of the nearly $5 billion a year stolen by employees is attributable to supervisory and executive personnel, in spite of generous fringe benefits and incentive programs aimed at motivating employees to be loyal and productive. In addition, large losses result from kickbacks, conflicts of interest, falsification of labor vouchers, sabotage, theft of company secrets, improper disposition of scrap, and damaged material.

Prosperity breeds dishonesty and neglect, whereas recession exposes losses and creates new threats, particularly on the white-collar level. Increased sales and profits during periods of prosperity mask flagrant manipulations which frequently cause taxes to be paid on nonexistent earnings. Periods of recession tend to flush out these malpractices and uncover other forms of dishonesty—for example, fraud resorted to by executives whose bonuses suddenly were eliminated, whose profit-sharing plans evaporated, whose stock options became valueless, or more drastically, whose stock options were financed with the aid of sizable bank loans that now must be met while the value of the stock is greatly depressed.

Another threat to business is posed by the man who devoted a lifetime to building his company and then sold it for stock which is now much lower in value. With the stock selling at only a fraction of its former equity, all he has left is an employment contract, his wits, and a desperate desire to recoup his loss. Under the circumstances, it may be easy for him to rationalize that he has been unfairly treated and then try to recoup his fortune at the company's expense.

The wave of corporate mergers often has a marked impact on dishonesty. Consequently, many mergers, instead of making a contribution, create a drain on corporate profits. Mergers and acquisitions lead to increased sales and, hopefully, increased profits, but may foster disloyalty and frustration. Some employees are frightened of being demoted or fired. Others expect wonderful things to happen; when the things that happen are not so wonderful, the employee becomes frustrated and angry. These feelings may lead to double dealing with vendors, sale of proprietary information, and other forms of disloyalty.

Publicity about telephone bugging, industrial spies and counterspies, and electronic snooping has needlessly diverted some executives from comprehending the real threat. Businessmen are far more likely to lose their secrets, money, and goods through their employees' dishonesty than by razzle-dazzle electronic spying.

Some executives assume that automation and computers will reduce the possibility of embezzlement because the machine is immune to corruption and temptation. However, human beings operate the equipment. If they deliberately distort or feed them incorrect information, the machines will digest mistakes, honest and dishonest, without knowing the difference.

The validity of figures is no better than the source, and knowledge of computer systems today is widespread enough so that numerous persons inside and outside the company may use the system's weaknesses for their own profit.

In addition to the vulnerability of the computer to fraud by dishonest employees, management is faced with two other major concerns. Countless companies are storing their vital information on tapes. In many cases the loss of tapes could be disastrous; at the very least, it could cost considerable time and money to reconstruct the data from raw material.

Access to tapes and tape libraries is easy for employees. The destruction of tapes, through carelessness or maliciousness, is equally easy and the culprit is virtually undetectable.

A data processing employee recently stole his company's master tape file of more than two million customers' names and sold them to a competitor. An employee of another company erased $192,000 worth of accounts receivables from tapes because he "just didn't feel like working."

The need to know what is really going on is highlighted when our management engineers undertake systems surveys and inventory control projects. In more than half of these cases, with no prior indication of dishonesty, sizable losses have been uncovered. They find falsification of records, inventory manipulation, and outright theft.

People have developed self-defeating rationalization into a highly sophisticated art. The National Council on Alcoholism knows this; people really do say, "I can take it or leave it alone." The Cancer Society is aware of it; people resist going to the doctor because they suspect that they are very sick and they fear that the doctor will confirm that suspicion. Businessmen have become masters of rationalization about business crime. One of the most prevalent devices employed to keep from looking at the truth is the conviction that business is victimized principally by offenses committed by outsiders.

In addressing a New York business group, former U.S. Attorney Robert Morgenthau did not argue against the proposition that business is the focal point for a lot of "outside" crime. He referred to "stock frauds and manipulation, tax evasion, embezzlement of corporate and pension funds, bribery and corruption, and many forms of consumer fraud." And then he suggested that a society that tolerates this kind of white-collar crime on a massive scale "can also expect crimes of violence."

Another powerful rationalization is rooted in the businessman's unfounded belief in the enormous efficacy of his anti-theft controls: "Our auditors check our controls and our protection department double-checks our employees, top to bottom. We are aware of everything that is going on. It can't happen here."

We run into another rationalization cherished by departmental managers. Few of them voice it baldly, but what they are saying is that *they* do not own the business, they are paid employees, and thus the stealing, deplorable as it may be, does not come out of their pockets. No, it does not come out of their pockets—not directly. But the emphasis nowadays is on results. A manager is judged by the numbers showing up on the bottom line. If steady dishonesty is magnifying costs and eroding profits in his operation, he will finally pay the price for it. The dishonesty, or at any rate the full extent of it, may not emerge; but what does become evident is that the particular manager has not been a profitable operator. Maybe he is thought to be "unlucky." No matter; he is replaced.

Often we confront the "I trust him implicitly; he's one of us" syndrome. We find this attitude among executives who think of their colleagues and high-ranking subordinates as if they were all members of the same club. A man of honor does not impute even the possibility of dishonesty to his fellow club member.

Well, there is a saying these days: "We have met the enemy and they are us." Today the community is faced with a new kind of thief. He graduated from college, and in many cases a very "good" college. He lives in a lovely home, has a fine family. His surface posture is upright in all of his dealings; he seems to be a respected member of the community. And yet this admirable, dependable person may turn out to be dishonest. As the Research Institute of America put it in a special report to its members, "The big steal is usually committed by a 'completely trustworthy' employee, the one the boss would trust with his wife. Insurance investigators find that behind the fantastic frauds and clever chicanery are open invitations to steal which top management does not perceive."

This high-level individual is not inherently more dishonest than the rank-and-file worker; but his opportunities are immeasurably greater, and he is protected by the "club ethic" which sees, hears, and speaks no evil of fellow members.

As a matter of fact, digressing from business for a moment, *clubs themselves* are far from immune from fraud. Not long ago the well-known Overseas Press Club notified its members that the board had voted to assess them up to $50 each because of the "urgent need" created by the discovery of an unexplained deficit in the books. As reported in the *New York Times:* "The deficit, apparently $110,000 but possibly including an additional $65,000 in 'questionable receivables' for which no reserve had been provided, had been announced after an emergency meeting of the board. . . ."

Often institutions that one would least expect have discovered that their trust is ill-founded. The Church of Jesus Christ of Latter Day Saints, more familiarly known as the Mormon Church, conveys to all a stern image of four-square rectitude. Certainly Mormons consider this so. Therefore it was with astonishment and dismay that officials admitted the church had been shorn of more than $600,000 by a "trusted church auditor" within a period of little more than one year. This devoted functionary turned out to have a previous conviction for embezzlement; and though higher officials of the Mormon Church had been unaware of this conviction, his probation report bore with it letters from six Mormon bishops and elders in the Salt Lake City area, asking for leniency.

Another form of rationalization is the hopeless shrug of the shoulders and comment that "they're going to steal from you anyway, there's nothing you can do about it."

We simply do not accept the proposition that nothing can be done. It can be done; we shall cite examples of its being done; and we can provide practical recommendations on how to control business dishonesty.

Of course the problem is not merely one of improvement of management practices. As a people we have drifted into a state bordering upon apathy toward dishonesty.

Morality has become a relative thing. Dishonesty, and acceptance of dishonesty, are widespread. Of course there are things that are still beyond the pale—crimes that we all abhor with equal vigor—but stealing from the company does not fall into this classification. Nobody feels sorry for the corporation. Or almost nobody. Sometimes even businessmen act as if they must suffer dishonesty as a natural concomitant of their enterprise.

Frequently businessmen *know they are being victimized*. In some cases the knowledge is vague. The manager is aware that there is stealing, but he does not know the extent of it, nor can he identify the thieves. As we look more closely into such situations, we often find that such vagueness and ignorance are *matters of choice*. The businessman prefers not to be told too much about the termites who are eating away the foundation of his company.

If he pinpoints dishonesty he will have to fire people, and finding replacements for certain jobs is difficult and expensive. Then there is also the feeling that the new people brought in as replacements will be just as bad as those he has fired. He may even have to face the fact that some people whom he likes and trusts very much have been taking advantage of him. This is embarrassing and unpleasant, and he emotionally withdraws from such a confrontation.

Finally, of course, there are the great tranquilizers: "We have set up a reserve" or "I'm insured." The insurance policies in the treasurer's files serve as sedation, a kind of soothing absolution from worry about fraud.

Very seldom does this businessman take a look at the escalating premiums paid for those policies. If he did, he might conclude that he is paying a pretty high price for this form of consolation.

The economist Sylvia Porter talked with Louis W. Niggeman, president of Fireman's Fund American Insurance Companies. She asked: "Isn't it true that we, the consumers, pay the bill for all this? Don't you pass it on to us?" Mr. Niggeman replied:

> Sure you pay and sure we pass it on. The insurance company is temporarily burdened with the cost of crime, but insurance eventually passes the cost on to the businessman in the form of increased premiums. The businessman in turn passes the cost on to the consumer via higher prices. You pay in the end.
>
> I would estimate that no more than 10 percent of those affected by criminal acts are adequately insured. It is no secret that some inadequately insured businesses in high-crime areas add to the price of their merchandise to offset the high cost of shoplifting and other forms of theft. This is another instance where the bill for crime is passed directly to the consumer.

Some businessmen brought face to face with these realities find it a lot tougher to continue relying on "I'm insured" as a source of peace of mind. But then there is the alternate reassurance: "The cost is passed on to the consumer."

Many businessmen take comfort in the fact that their competitors suffer similar losses. Rather than doing something about the situation, they pass the increased costs on to the consumer. But how much cost can be passed on to the consumer? Is there no limit? We are all consumers. And recent housewives' boycotts of high-priced beef demonstrate conclusively that "the con-sumer" is not a magic camel whose back has no breaking point.

If your competitor is determined to root out the causes and correct his problems, not only does he show a greater profit but he is able to pass on the savings to the consumer. This has been demonstrated in super-markets and department stores. If you do nothing about it, the consumer soon lets you know—in ways that hurt —whose approach he prefers.

Furthermore, many firms jolted by huge losses and cancelled policies become better insurance risks because they are made aware of their vulnerability and take positive measures to limit or nullify it.

There is another way in which executives disassociate themselves from the exorbitant cost of business dishon-esty. Typically, one manager told us, "My value to the company is my creativity. I try to think broadly, think positively. If I am going to sit around and brood about every salesman who pads his expense account and every machine operator who cheats on the incentive plan or takes a power tool home in his lunch box, I'm through. They don't pay me to be a cop."

"They don't pay me to be a cop." The idea is that, if cops are needed, pay them; but don't take up the time and drain off the creative energy of high-powered management on the policy level.

Maybe the "cops" are already on the payroll, super-visors who are supposed to enforce honesty. During a survey at a national metals company we arrived at the plant one morning a few minutes before the first shift reported. We noticed deep tracks in the snow from the shipping dock to a remote area of the fence, indicating that mechanized material handling equip-ment had been used to convey a heavy load there. The first-shift foreman reported that a sizable quantity of copper and brass was missing. We spoke with the night-shift foreman. He said, "I'm with this firm twenty-four years—eleven years as foreman—I know there is sizable stealing going on, but that's not my job. I'm paid for production." He added, "Besides, there are very tough people on this graveyard shift, and I'm tired of being threatened and having my tires slashed."

The most sweeping marketing plan, the most radically improved product, the most innovative simplification of manufacturing, the acquisition of the most promising subsidiary—all these are being nullified today by employee dishonesty.

Some businessmen *are* doing something about the dishonesty drain, and their successful efforts show up in successful performance.

3 INTELLIGENCE, YES; MAGIC, NO!

Many businessmen have a Maginot Line complex. They install a few protective measures—and assume that they are secure. This can be the point at which they are most vulnerable. This chapter examines the most harmful assumptions about safety that a businessman can make.

Every day the manager confronts massive difficulties and responsibilities. Each day brings new worries, new decisions, new demands. Coping as he does with equations in which all elements are variables, it is little wonder that the executive yearns for a little assurance in at least some areas.

The most sophisticated executive may lull himself into a false sense of security by almost superstitious belief in the "magic" offered by certain practices and symbols.

In anthropological writings are found interesting parallels between the rites and beliefs of primitive people and the practices followed by some modern businessmen. Sir James Frazer, in *The Golden Bough,* tells us that on the island of Timor the high priest never quits the temple while war is being waged. He keeps the fire going. The temple is always open to his tribesmen; if they do not find him in residence, disaster will follow.

Ridiculous? But is it any more of a delusion than that of the company president who says: "I know everything that goes on in this organization. My door is always open"? In one corporation blessed with such an "open door" policy we uncovered a department head who was sitting on a desperate fraud situation. Referring to his president whose "door was always open," the department head said, "Did he think I was going to walk in there and tell him I was short a hundred thousand?" Nevertheless, this "open door" was the president's "magic" against loss.

At this point one may well protest that every manager must take chances, that risk is inherent in any business operation.

True. As Dr. Bela Gold of Case Western Reserve University puts it, in talking of expenditure for Research and Development: "Let's say that only 5 percent of R & D projects work out. So if the manager says *no* to them all, he's 95 percent right; and how right can a man expect to be? *But,* if he does this, his business will die."

The risks that a good manager takes are *calculated* risks. Maybe he doesn't always calculate his risks accurately, but at least he knows he is taking them. It is the uncalculated risk, the risk to which management blinds itself by creating an illusion of safety, that leads to dishonesty, corruption, significant loss, and possibly ultimate calamity.

There are five "magic" beliefs which have, over and over again, lulled businessmen into a suicidal illusion of safety:

- "We can't become too concerned. It's normal for our industry. We have to close our eyes, they all do it."
- The belief in "foolproof methods" that are supposed

to forestall all possibility of dishonesty.

* The belief that "the team spirit" makes employees, high and low, think only of the good of the organization.
* The belief that thorough investigation is not necessary because you grew up together.
* The belief in the "authority of the uniform"—that guards are immutably trustworthy.

There are few things more mutually painful to consultant and client than the shattering of an illusion. When the illusion is based on management's strong belief in the total honesty of a trusted employee, the realization is not only distressing, but extremely difficult to accept.

Audrey Blue Sportswear got its start during the dreary tail end of the great Depression. Mrs. Walter Berman cut and sewed blouses on her own machine in the Berman flat. Berman traveled the subway to sell the blouses. The product caught on. Berman rented some office space. His first employee was Leah Metz—in her early twenties, unmarried, physically unprepossessing, and socially awkward, but a dedicated worker. Leah Metz grew indispensable to the business. In many ways she *was* the business. Her title? Well, Leah never really had a title. Executive secretary, maybe; girl Friday, perhaps; but really something more than those designations imply.

There wasn't much money coming in during those early days. After Leah paid the most pressing bills (often skipping her own modest salary), she divided what was left and put it into envelopes: "Mrs. Berman really needs a winter coat and you agreed—and here is your *allowance*." Walter Berman would remember nostalgically that his envelope was usually pretty thin.

Audrey Blue Sportswear grew to where it was (and

is) doing about $15 million in business. The economy
and the women's wear business went through immense
changes. But one thing did not change. Leah Metz
could still be counted on to handle everything from
the Berman personal checkbook to serious disputes
with suppliers, all with the same quiet efficiency and
devotion. For all this Leah was paid a good, if not
princely, wage. She had never married. Her life was
the company.

Over the years Walter Berman began to get a little
concerned. Manufacturing and selling sportswear is
not a tidy business; even so, sometimes he got to thinking that, with the kind of volume he was doing, there
ought to be more money coming out at the bottom line.
So Berman talked to us. When we heard about Leah,
we wanted to talk a little more about her. But this
was not for Mr. Berman. "You can't be suggesting . . . !"
We were not suggesting. We were only asking at this
stage.

Subsequently, Walter Berman retired to a less active role as chairman of the board, and his son Arthur
became president of Audrey Blue. Arthur Berman came
to us. Profit margins were still unsatisfactory in spite
of increased sales. Now we took a closer look at Leah
Metz. To be brief, while we will never know the full
extent of what Leah Metz took from the company and
the Berman family, we do know that it is well over
a quarter of a million dollars. She invested more
than $100,000 in real estate, mostly around Fort Lau-
derdale, Florida.

Walter Berman's life-long illusion was gone—"My
God, you can't trust *anybody.*"

We don't believe that "you can't trust anybody." We
cannot subscribe to something else that Walter Berman
said: "No one could have treated Leah better than I
did." You are not treating people well when you *make
it easy for them to become thieves.*

Leah Metz told us that she learned to handle all the bosses' expenses, personal bills, trips, charitable contributions, as well as weekend cash sales—which made it all too easy for her, first for the benefit of the Bermans and then for herself. What made her do it? As the years slipped by Leah began to feel that "I made Berman what he is," and yet had little to show for it.

Walter Berman's trust in this faithful employee was emotional. Such an approach to choosing a key subordinate is regarded with indulgent condescension by managers of a more modern stripe. The sophisticated manager places confidence in people—after all, he has to—but he bases it on *facts*. And yet this manager can be just as prone to the dangerous illusion of safety as the old-fashioned boss.

There are other dangerous illusions. Maddox Electric is a corporation with annual sales in the billions. The Maddox Small Appliance Division sells strictly through authorized distributors. Since this is the backbone of the division's marketing approach, there was understandable concern in the sales office when a call came in from an irate distributor. His opening sally was, "If you people are dropping me as a distributor, you might at least have the courtesy to let me know about it."

A hurried check of the books. Then, "Kemp, we've always had the best of working relationships with you and we have no thought of dropping you. Where did you get that idea?"

Kemp was not appeased: "Then how the hell do you explain the fact that my competitor down the street has your new line listed in his catalog, and I haven't been posted yet?"

It must be a mistake, Kemp was told. But Kemp was sure that if there was a mistake, he was not making it. He said, "Why don't you place an order with my competitor like my ex-customer did?" Maddox placed an order and got the merchandise; they placed an order for another item, and got it. The competitor was selling merchandise from the new lines that had not yet been released by the company to any of its dealers.

"It beats me," said the Vice-President of Administration as we were discussing the problem in his office. "As you can well imagine, we keep this stuff under the tightest security. And we can't understand how it was done." He underscored the security setup: "It's complete. A nine-foot heavyweight link fence, with one access; a captain of the guard always on duty; full alarm system, constantly monitored, and twenty-seven uniformed guards covering each shift."

We asked for the employment applications of the twenty-seven guards. We were told, "No, we don't have employment applications because we use an outside guard service." We then asked for the names and addresses of the guards, and he said there was no such record in personnel, that the supervisor of the guards on duty kept the record of the guards' names and time worked. He said he saw no reason why they should have backgrounds on the guards—their employer takes care of the whole thing. Here, a company turns over the keys to their premises to people completely unknown to them, yet they would not trust their own employees who may have been with them for many years and perhaps earning three times the wages the guards receive. You give them a uniform, a badge, and perhaps a gun—and you go home to sleep. And, what do you think they may be doing?

We eventually learned that the sergeant of the guards on the night shift, who had a master key to the warehouse in which the new merchandise was stored, was working in collusion with the routeman servicing the food-vending machines. When the routeman arrived to service the machines at his regularly scheduled time, 3:00 A.M., the sergeant had pulled the items from the new lines for which the routeman had solicited orders the previous day. The merchandise was being systematically removed in the routeman's truck.

For most of us, when we were children, the policeman on the beat was a stern, straightforward, yet understanding symbol of reliable authority. Perhaps this is why so many grownups still subconsciously equate a uniform and a badge with rectitude. But just open to the classified section of your newspaper. Scan the listings under "Guards." A typical sampling:

GUARDS
Full & Part Time/All shifts
Fast hire. No experience required.
Must be 21 or over.

It is an unskilled industry, with a high turnover rate. It attracts retired people, moonlighters, disabled persons, and many who just can't get any other job. Nevertheless, it has grown into a multi-million dollar industry because of the demand resulting from businessmen's desperation.

Awareness of the risks it is taking will eventually force the guard industry to revitalize and to upgrade the caliber and training of the people they employ. However, it is up to you to check the individuals' backgrounds, qualifications, and performance. Guards should be accountable to you on daily activity and findings, regardless of who they report to in their own companies. It is unreasonable to expect that uniformed guards, unchecked and uncontrolled by you, are going to be titans of integrity.

This overview of uniformed services is neither an indictment nor a reflection on the professional directors of security. Many of these persons have police, military, or government related training and are not only highly qualified, but have special skills in public relations and business administration.

When you talk of *systems,* businessmen's eyes light up! Millions in fraud go undetected, because management is genuflecting before the glittering idol of the "foolproof system."

One case of the folly of the foolproof system is drawn from the files of Norman Jaspan Associates on a large low-priced shoe chain in a midwestern city. In most of its elements the case is typical of many.

It developed the way most cases do. Emil Orson, president of Orson Shoe Shops, came away worried from a conference with his controller. They couldn't put their fingers on anything—and yet, with the volume that Orson Shops seemed to be doing, earnings were just not as good as they should be.

When we first met Orson, we began asking questions about how the branches were operated and controlled. When we got to stock controls, Orson shrugged: "You can look into it as much as you want, but it would be a waste of time. About a year ago we put in—although it involves a lot of time and effort—a perpetual inventory system. Each withdrawal from stock is noted on a stock record card, and we maintain a running balance. And we make unannounced checks. No serious discrepancies—it comes to less than one percent. Here, you can look at the figures."

We took Orson's word for the figures. We were more interested in his faith in the perpetual inventory system. He had not said, "It's foolproof," but that is what he meant.

We picked a downtown store doing a large volume and visited it, just to ask the people who worked there some questions. We were soon in a warm and animated chat with the cashier. Of course, we asked no questions bearing directly on the possibility of fraud. As Damon Runyon's first-person character once remarked, "I do not ask him the question as he may think I wish to know the answer." As we chatted, the lady was sympathetic with the problems of the Orson Shoe Shops' top management; free with inside tips on how to build high volume in a downtown store, and effusive in her offers of cooperation . . . "Any help I can give you. . . ." This was a departure from pattern. Most people, even with absolutely nothing to hide, are inclined to become a little reticent when approached by outside consultants brought in by the management to look into a problem.

But, above all, the cashier was unflagging in her praise for her boss—the store manager, Mr. Kay. Kay was a fine man: generous with his employees, understanding of their problems; important socially in the suburb where he lived, and well-known and respected among the businessmen in that part of the city.

That last piece of information we had already learned. In that part of town the term "business" covered a rather large area. The shop was on Market Street. It stood on a respectable block. But just to the south, the proportion of bars and cocktail lounges, second-rate hotels, and poolrooms grew steadily larger. And it turned out that Mr. Kay had a few side business interests of his own. He could get you jewelry, furniture, furs at outstanding bargain prices. ("It's a steal" is sometimes more than a figurative term.) He could arrange for you to have a drink and even a party after hours. And, if you were just visiting town, lonely, and well-recommended, Mr. Kay could get you a girl.

But did all this mean that Kay was defrauding the shoe company? Not positively; but for us the question was beginning to shift from "Is he doing it?" to "*How* is he doing it?" After all, there was the foolproof perpetual inventory. Kay's store was showing performance and a profit. And, with these people working so closely together, wouldn't somebody become wise to what was going on?

As the case developed, the answer to the last question was simple: they were *all* in on it. Kay maintained his own controls, using a seniority system. The cashier was permitted to keep the first $25 she took in every day. Three senior clerks were privileged to steal $15 every day. People with less tenure were allowed to steal smaller amounts.

And the inventory system was a pushover—particularly for a team led by a man with such energy and inventiveness as Mr. Kay, and particularly because management had lulled itself into the illusion of security. A $24 unit sale would be rung up as three $8 transactions; shoes would be switched from box to box; empty shoe boxes decorated the shelves (to be dutifully counted in the surprise inventory checks); and always the running stock cards balanced out. Really, it was easy.

People bent on collusion can beat any system. And the more a business is oriented to figures on paper instead of to human beings, the more prone it is to dishonesty. In *The Folklore of Management*, Clarence Randall issues a heartfelt warning to "fine old institutions with great names and impressive records" in which "the strength of the balance sheet is merely a facade that conceals the decay within."

We cannot banish illusion from our lives. If we did, existence would be an arid exercise. But the businessman can help himself to avoid dangerous illusions of security which can undermine his business.

The business manager should treat himself to an occasional *inventory of opinions*. Ask yourself what you currently think about the methods by which your business is being run, and about the people who run it.

Then ask these questions:

• How much of what I think is based on *fact,* and how much on the way I *hope* things are going?
• How old are my facts? When was the last time I thoroughly investigated this situation? (Sometimes an honest answer can be surprising.)
• What is the breaking point of each of my most trusted associates? What is *my* breaking point? The last question, when faced honestly can lead to some interesting speculations. For we all have a breaking point.

There is a story (probably apocryphal) about Abraham Lincoln as a young lawyer in Springfield. Another lawyer approached Lincoln and asked him to fix a case. He offered $20.

Lincoln said, "No."

The other lawyer said, "I'll make it $50."

Lincoln replied, "Not interested."

The other lawyer then offered $100—and with that, Lincoln rose and threw him bodily out of the office.

Some time later, on the circuit, the would-be briber approached Lincoln and asked, "Why did you suddenly use me with such violence?"

And Lincoln answered, "Because you were coming close to my price."

Look at everyone around you as if he had just come into your business, and as if you were about to entrust him with a thousand dollars of your own money. Don't relax common-sense precautions just because a certain man or woman has been around a long time. After all, *thinking* in terms of favorites leads to playing favorites —bad management practice in any respect.

Check unpredictably, *but check in depth.* A good spot check is not to ask questions, it is to see for yourself. For example, in conducting inventory, make sure that *merchandise* is being tallied, not cards, labels, or even boxes.

Imagine yourself in a sensitive position, *and figure out how you would defraud the company.*

The Institute of Internal Auditors reported that one of its members was having trouble convincing management that its internal controls were weak. So, having let one man—the treasurer—in on the secret, he conducted an experiment.

He drew checks for renovation work that was never done; he even made the payee's name the name of the president's assistant spelled backwards. The checks went through. He sent invoices, plainly stamped PAID, through the bookkeeping process a second time. They were paid twice, without comment.

He requested checks for substantial amounts, bypassing most of the so-called controls. The request simply read "Rush check for $5,000, payable to Company X—invoice will follow." The request would be signed with the initials of a trusted employee. No difficulty at all.

Samples of checks were taken from the bookkeeping area (they were kept in unlocked files) and sent to the check signer with a typed note: "This is a replacement for check No. __ which I have destroyed; payee was wrong—rush." Even though the process required several people to make significant adjustments, no one asked any questions.

Management agreed to take a fresh look at its controls.

Here is a guideline we prepared for members of the National Association of Wholesaler-Distributors as an aid to pinpointing areas of high vulnerability and points of loss. You may find that many of the questions can help you to make a realistic risk inventory of your own operation.

SHORTAGE CONTROL CHECKLIST

I. Employee Controls

    1. When a new employee is hired do we:
        Check references of all previous employers? ___
        Require bonding form to be completed? _____
        Check financial status? _____
        Require photo of employee? _____

    2. Are ambiguous replies followed up by phone calls? ___

    3. a. Are employees covered by a fidelity bond?
        All _____ Some _____ None _____
      b. Are employees aware that they are bonded? _____

    4. Approximately how many employees have been discharged for dishonesty, violation of rules, falsification of records, and other malpractices in the past three years in the following job categories?

        Supervisory _____
        Executive _____
        Purchasing _____
        Salesmen _____
        Warehouse employees _____
        Office employees _____
        Shipping Dept. employees _____
        Truck drivers _____

    5. Underlying factors which we consider of major importance in controlling losses that are not reflected on our books:

        ( ) Supervisory failures
        ( ) Double standards
        ( ) Excessive exposure of assets
        ( ) Inadequate controls
        ( ) Low morale
        ( ) Policy shortcomings

    6. When dishonesty or other serious irregularities are uncovered, does our organization usually take corrective action by:
    (check applicable answers)

        ( ) Dismissing suspected employee at once
        ( ) Notifying the police

( ) Turning the entire matter over to the bonding company
( ) Determining full extent of losses incurred
( ) Determining if any procedures were at fault, and correcting them
( ) Ascertaining range of related malpractices
( ) Setting up tests (e.g., "created error" programs, surprise audits, spot checks and searches) to confirm suspicions

7. When employees who work in sensitive areas go on vacation do we ensure that:
    Records are updated? _____
    Department head has checked work schedule? ____

    Where needed, an audit is completed? _____

8. Do any employees perform outside work in which products stocked by our company could be used? _____

9. Are references checked or demanded on:
    Guards from outsides agencies? _____
    Truck drivers? (On rentals?)_____
    Temporary clericals? _____
    Temporary labor? _____

II. Inventory Control

1. How often do we take a physical inventory of stock on hand?

    Annually _____   Semi-annually _____
    Quarterly _____   Other (Specify) _____

2. What was our inventory shrinkage as a percent of sales in our last three inventories?

    _____   _____   _____

3. Do mysterious disappearances tend to be concentrated in certain product classifications? _____ (Yes, No, or Don't Know) If answer is Yes, list the classification or classifications most subject to such losses.

    _____
    _____
    _____

4. Rate in order of importance the areas and operations we

consider most vulnerable to inventory shrinkage by in-
serting the numbers 1 through 10 below.

( ) Receiving
( ) Cash sales
( ) Packing
( ) Order picking
( ) Customer returns
( ) Salvage & scrap
( ) Shipping & delivery
( ) Employee purchases
( ) Full-case storage
( ) Other (Specify)

5. Are copies of purchase orders furnished to the Receiving
Department? _____

6. Are complete counts taken of all incoming merchandise? _____

7. Are signed receiving reports prepared for all goods
received? _____

8. Are receiving reports pre-numbered, and is a copy kept
in the Receiving Department? _____

9. Are receivers occasionally required to take a "blind"
count, with their total matched against the invoice or
packing slip by a second party? _____

10. Are returned goods properly accounted for, and
promptly restocked and posted to inventory control
records? _____

11. When returned goods are tallied, is a copy of the tally
sheet attached to the credit memo? _____

12. Are all invoices and shipping tickets pre-numbered? ___

13. Are all unusable invoices filed with other invoices in
numerical sequence? _____

14. Are small and valuable items stored in safeguarded areas
separated from customer and employee traffic? _____

15. Is all merchandise moved from dock to truck checked by
an independent party other than the person filling or
trucking the order? _____

16. On goods delivered off the dock, are sales slips matched
to shipping checker copies of order prior to billing or
filing? _____

17. Are perpetual inventory records maintained in ink? Are erasures prohibited and corrections initialed by a supervisor? _____

18. Is the physical inventory taken by two-man teams (caller and writer), with a third man (checker) verifying the counts? _____

19. When the perpetual inventory records are corrected on the basis of physical inventory counts, is management advised of the discrepancies? _____ Are the discrepancy figures translated into dollars? _____

III. Physical Controls and Building Safeguards

1. Do we have effective exit security to discourage employees from taking company merchandise home? _____

2. Can employees come and go as they please during lunch and relief periods, free from observation and control by supervisors? _____

3. Are the stock areas subdivided and casual wandering prohibited? _____

4. Do we spot check our waste collection and trash disposal? _____

5. Do we have a master key or duplicate that will open every locker on the premises, and are periodic inspections made? _____

6. Are all windows barred or screened, including those on the upper floors? _____

7. Do porters and cleaning people work unobserved, after hours, and do they have access to valuable merchandise? _____

8. Do the salesmen have free run of the stock areas? _____

9. Are all window and door locks checked nightly? _____

10. Is the employee parking area located away from the loading dock? _____

11. Do any employees work alone in the building after hours or on weekends? _____

12. Are strangers in the warehouse area, including outside truckers, challenged by employees or supervisors? _____

13. Do we have an effective alarm system to protect the premises after hours? _____

14. Does the alarm system have separate circuits to permit some work areas to function while others are closed? _____

15. Does a member of top management get an independent report of the daily opening and closing times of the distribution center? _____

IV. Cash and Other Bookkeeping Controls

1. Is the mail opened by someone other than cashier or receivable personnel? _____

2. Is a record prepared by the person opening the mail of the money and checks received, and is this record used by someone independent of the cashier to verify the amount recorded and deposited? _____

3. If a cash register, counter sales slips, collectors' receipts, etc. are used in providing the cash receipts, is the proof made by an employee independent of the cashier? _____

4. Are each day's receipts deposited intact and without delay? _____

5. Is the responsibility for the receipt and deposit of cash centralized in as few individuals as possible? _____

6. Does someone independent of the cashier occasionally make a surprise check of the items in the deposit against the cash-receipts record and deposit ticket after the deposit has been prepared? _____

7. Do cash customers always get a register receipt or authenticated sales slip? _____

8. Is the register or cash drawer always locked when not attended? _____

9. a. Do you occasionally "salt" the register or cash drawer and note if the overage is reported? _____
   b. What is the frequency per month of:
      Overages _____   Shortages _____

10. Does the authorization for adjustments in the customary discount allowances need tightening? _____

11. Are all canceled checks examined for authenticity? _____

12. Are all incoming checks stamped "For Deposit" before turning them over to the bookkeeper? _____

13. Are receiving reports and B/L matched to purchase orders and invoices *and carefully examined* prior to payment? _____

14. Are periodic statements furnished to all customers? ____

15. Has the bank been instructed in writing to cash no checks payable to the company? _____

16. Are voided checks mutilated to prevent re-use and kept on file? _____

17. Are disbursements made only on the basis of approved vouchers with supporting data attached? _____

18. Are the supporting data and approvals on the vouchers reviewed by the check signer at time of signature? _____

19. Are cash receipts mingled with the petty cash fund? ___

20. Are petty cash disbursements evidenced by supporting data properly approved? _____

21. Are the bank statements reconciled by employees who do not participate in the receipt or disbursement of cash and do not sign checks? _____

22. Are bank statements and canceled checks obtained by the person making the reconciliation directly from the mail room or the bank? _____

4 THOSE GULLIBLE CONGLOMERATES

Big or small, commercial or institutional—every organization is a target for crime. Here's how dishonest employees are exploiting a variety of businesses and public enterprises.

It takes courage, initiative, and vision to build a successful giant conglomerate. But the requisite long view may contain myopic spots that blind the eyes of management to fraud of impressive proportions. And it is not just a matter of the eyes, but the ears as well. Often the conglomerate acquires highly complex subsidiaries whose operations are understood only vaguely by the men at the top. The subsidiary operates autonomously, at least for a while. There is little communication.

One U.S. company, starting in the burgeoning field of automation, made acquisitions at a rapid rate. Some of these were pretty far afield, both geographically and in terms of the kind of business the subsidiary was in. Not long ago this company—we'll call it Discovery Industries—decided that things were going to boom in Alaska and the western part of Canada as the new oil fields came under exploitation. So, to get in on the ground floor, Discovery Industries bought a large Canadian construction firm, Caribou Ltd.

Caribou's management presented a glowing picture of the prospects that were in store, if Discovery would come through initially with the right kind of backing. The picture looked good to Discovery's top brass, and they cooperated by supporting Caribou to the hilt. There was no doubt that Caribou was aggressively going after really big jobs. Into Discovery Industries headquarters there began to flow copies of contracts in the $25 million range. They were fixed-cost contracts, which gave Caribou every assurance that the jobs would be done at a profit. Nobody at Discovery fully comprehended some of the highly technical information coming down from the northland, but Caribou had landed plenty of jobs, was reporting spectacular progress on a number of them, and there was every reason to believe that they would go right on growing.

Discovery Industries helped Caribou sign up some top U.S. firms who were also interested in the region. These clients, too, were intrigued by the construction company's willingness to take a chance by bidding low—and by its reports of progress. Executives who visited the sites could not, of course, tell precisely what had been accomplished; but the explanations were cogent and encouraging, and there were certainly plenty of men and equipment on the job.

But things were not as they seemed with Caribou Ltd. First of all, Caribou was winning contracts with some spectacularly low bids. Occasionally somebody at Discovery would wonder if the subsidiary could *really* make a profit on a given job, but he would conclude that "they know what they are doing." Caribou's management knew what it was doing, all right; but what it was doing was not work. On a good many jobs the subcontractor was deliberately bidding low, winning the assignment, pocketing the advance money, and then backlogging the job without doing anything further.

The existence of the contract was enough to persuade Discovery Industries to come through with bigger chunks of financial backing.

On other jobs Caribou would move in a different direction. Men, materials, and equipment would be moved onto the site before engineering designs and plans had been completed. Caribou was able to get customers to come through with not only the down payment, but progress payments as well. As a typical example, the contractor told one U.S. refinery: "We've had 200 men on the job for the past three months. We're 30 percent completed." Actually only 5 percent had been completed, but the refinery paid on the basis of 30 percent. Of course not all customers were so naive, but Caribou made liberal use of bribes to convince certain managers in some of the client companies that things really *were* the way Caribou said they were. The contractor grew so bold that it was reporting significant construction work during months when the weather is so cold that one cannot even drive a stake into the ground.

At Discovery Industries there was elation over the success of this acquisition. The reports looked wonderful. In September of its first year of operation as a subsidiary, Caribou presented a financial statement (as yet unaudited) projecting a net profit of $4 to $5 million. But as the months dragged on, this rosy picture began to turn a little yellow at the edges. By December the projected profit had shrunk to $100,000. By January a $1 million loss was projected. A month later Discovery management was staring at the imminent prospect of a loss of more than $3 million.

And what of the managers of Caribou Ltd.? Obviously they knew that the bubble had to burst sometime; they milked the parent company and the customers for everything that they could get—and then they scattered all over the world. Discovery Industries is still trying to cope with the reverberations.

For the conglomerate that is aggressively acquiring companies there are serious dangers. Distance can lend enchantment. Technical language can conceal the embezzlement of millions of dollars. Reports that make everything look good on paper can be a seductive trap.

Another problem facing the conglomerate that acquires a going business is that, in some cases, they are buying little more than total dependence upon one man. The conglomerate's management doesn't know the business; and there may really be only one individual who *does* know. The parent company may find that the tables are turned and that it is depending upon this one man. This can lead to some bizarre results.

For example, there is the case of Walter Slavin. Slavin has been with the Casimir Company for twenty-four years, working his way up from yard hand to general manager. He provided the drive and savvy that really built the business, which is principally involved in producing the steel members that are encased in concrete for such structures as the supporting piers of high-speed roadways.

Slavin's boss, Ernest Casimir, is past sixty. When Casimir retires, the business will pass to heirs who have little interest in it or knowledge of it. So Slavin goes to work to find a buyer for the business. He reasons that he can win himself a generous finder's fee plus a substantial contract for far more than he is making now.

Walter Slavin's search narrows down to one growing conglomerate, FTL, which is eager to expand into the construction field. Included in the negotiations with FTL is a finder's fee and a ten-year contract at $100,-000 per year. Slavin will make more than a million dollars out of the deal over the next decade—that is, if the deal goes through.

However, now there is a problem. The whole building industry is going sour as recession spreads. FTL is showing signs of backing off. Slavin becomes a little desperate. He is so close to success that he can taste it—but it looks as if all his hard work may go for nothing. FTL must be reassured that the Casimir Company is recession-proof. So Slavin uses his unique position to falsify figures, inflate inventory, create nonexistent backlogs of business. He works assiduously at this, and his skill is rewarded. FTL finally closes the deal.

Everything is fine for a while. The conglomerate leaves Slavin to run the business and sits back to enjoy the anticipated results. But the results are not there. A modest amount of inquiry shows that all was not as it appeared to be when the deal was consummated. The unhappy conglomerate is asking questions of Slavin—questions like, "How could you be $1 million off on a $3 million inventory?" Not surprisingly, the possibility of fraud creeps into management's mind. Slavin's answers are oblique and noncommital.

Now the parent company is faced with the dilemma of what to do about Slavin. Should they pursue the allegations of fraud? Should they fire him? If they do, who is going to run the business? FTL has no idea. So they come up with an ingenious solution. They go to Walter Slavin and say: "Something is wrong. At the very least this is a less profitable company than we were led to believe. So we want to renegotiate our contract with you. In fact, we insist upon it." The end result is that Slavin's compensation is reduced to $50,000 a year. He is out $500,000. But he is still running the business.

At this point it may not astonish the reader to learn

that losses continue at the Casimir Company. Now the losses take a different form: $100,000 worth of steel leaves the plant, but only $60,000 worth arrives on the job. What is happening to the rest of it? Slavin shrugs. He doesn't know.

But of course Slavin does know. He has not taken his drastic reduction in compensation lying down. He is getting his money back in another way—by fraud. Under-the-table arrangements with contractors, dummy suppliers, black-market sales of Casimir products—Slavin has become a large-scale business thief.

Of course this might have been predicted. The fantastic element is that FTL would set up a situation in which such a culmination is almost inevitable. But, from the conglomerate's point of view, what else could they do? When they bought the smaller company they really bought nothing but the brains and experience of one man. Gradually closed out from viable options by their ignorance of the business they have acquired, the conglomerate finds itself sitting with a losing hand which it has dealt itself.

Here is another case: An executive spent twenty-five years with an electronics company that was taken over in a merger. This was the only business he knew. He had helped to build it and now the company was sold. He was downgraded to line supervisor, became frustrated, and turned opportunist.

What did this man do? He set up his own business. He sold the company's dies and equipment for scrap, and bought them up secretly. He contacted the company's customers and wooed away its engineers and sales personnel. Subcontractors helped him to get started. His friends in the front office gave him confidential information on contracts and bids—proving that your own employees often can be your strongest competitors.

Sometimes we come upon a complex form of fraud that we might call theft by litigation. This not only can be extremely costly; it is almost always particularly painful because it involves the treachery of well-paid and highly trusted employees.

It happened recently to a worldwide chemical giant, one of whose divisions manufactures synthetic fibers. This synthetics division used in its factories certain machinery and processes supplied by an organization that we shall call United Milling Machinery, Inc. United Milling machines were instrumental in the production of a strong, nearly indestructible synthetic thread. But for some time the United Milling equipment had been presenting a problem. The synthetic yarn that it produced was so tough that, as it ran through the processing phases of the machine, the metal parts of the device were rapidly worn away. The United Milling machines were breaking down often, causing serious production delays as service crews arrived from United headquarters, and as machine parts were occasionally shipped back to the factory.

The synthetics manufacturer was becoming more and more unhappy with the situation. There was talk of dropping United (in spite of its possession of certain exclusive processes and patents) and seeking another supplier whose equipment might not be as efficient but which might be more rugged. Naturally, United reacted in alarm, asking for time to straighten out the situation.

Breakdowns continued; and now the chemical firm, reluctant to drop an old supplier who had given considerable satisfaction in the past, made a proposal. They said to United, in effect: "We can give you more time to develop a stronger machine, but only if the down-time on the present machines is cut drastically. As it stands now, we have to wait too long while your service people come to make the repairs. Let's agree on a procedure that makes sense for both of us. We will send our engineers into your plant to learn how to make repairs on the devices. This way we can conduct our own maintenance and keep the machines in running order for acceptable periods of time."

United agreed. The technical people went into the United plant to study the operation and were able to come up with a reasonably efficient means of maintaining the United devices on the site. Everything seemed fine, for the time being.

Eight months later the chemical firm was astounded when United's lawyers instituted suit for $50 million. The complaint was that the larger organization had stolen certain highly valuable processes from United and used them to branch out into a new area of the market. The plaintiff alleged that the thefts had been carried out by the chemical firm's engineers on their visits to the United plant, and that those thefts had been undertaken at the express orders of the engineers' employer. The defendant company replied that its engineers had visited the supplier, under agreement, *only* to learn how to repair the machines, *not* to learn anything about the fabricating process. An important item of the defense case would obviously be the trip sheets routinely filled out by these engineers every week.

And here is where the chemical manufacturer had a shock. For the trip sheets that had been filled out by four of the firm's engineers *did* support the plaintiff's contention that the engineers were working under instructions to learn how to make certain items. A major investigation was launched. No evidence could be found that anybody had issued such instructions to the engineers. It became more and more apparent that the trip sheets had been deliberately doctored to falsify the purpose of the plant visits. Who had done the doctoring? Somebody in the records section? No; the sheets had been altered by the engineers themselves.

By this time Norman Jaspan Associates had been called into the case. We found that the engineers had been approached by United people with bribes and promises of much larger bribes if they would fake the trip sheets, and if they would testify on trial that they had indeed been sent onto the supplier's premises to learn the supplier's secrets. Of course these engineers would be instantly fired; but this transitory embarrassment would be compensated for by large sums taken from the enormous claim that United confidently expected to win.

Here is a case in which normal security methods (and this synthetics manufacturer maintains quite an elaborate system of self-protection) failed totally to cover a loophole. In the interests of doing business fairly and profitably, any company must work in harmony and cooperation with its suppliers and customers. In this instance, trusted employees were lured into selling out their employer, and a generous effort at wholehearted cooperation was twisted into an extremely dangerous device for fraud. The engineers' trip sheets were part of what seemed to be a reasonable self-protective procedure; what the chemical company left out of the equation was the full realization of the boundless potential for human avarice.

When a good professional football quarterback sees that the opposition is using a zone pass defense, he tries to "hit the seams" in the zone, to pass to the spots where responsibility for coverage shifts between one defensive back and another. There are "seams" in the defense against fraud, sloppy areas, points of transfer, unglamorous parts of the operation that most members of top management find too boring to look at. Like a pro quarterback picking apart a zone defense, adroit business thieves exploit these "seams" to the tune of hundreds of millions of dollars per year. Here is a story of how shrewd operators found each other and were able to penetrate a seam in a corporation.

Elmer Deane was distribution manager for a manufacturer of consumer paper products doing $400 million in business per year. Elmer had an important job—responsibility for shipment of the company's merchandise from factories to warehouses to distributors. Yet his responsibility was not looked upon as one of the "glamour" jobs. He was paid $16,000 a year. Deane's aspirations and tastes ran far beyond this sum.

Leo Corbett got into the warehouse business, not through any lifelong affinity or experience, but rather through political pull. The Air Force had abandoned a field in his area. Several of the hangars were near a railroad siding, and Corbett was able to rent this facility for very little money. Next he lured away the manager from a large and prosperous warehouse a few blocks away, and he was off and running. Soon the other warehouse fell upon tough times.

Corbett could do all right as a legitimate warehouseman, but that is not where his interests lay. Supported by the expertise of his manager, who fell right in with this scheme of things, Corbett was soon cutting corners. Claims were entered that the railroad damaged goods in transit; the Corbett warehouse maintained a special floor full of damaged material, and this stuff was pulled out over and over again to show to the inspectors. Of course this practice required a little bribery, a little collusion; for instance, duplicate altered bills were needed from the railway clerk. All that could be arranged.

But when Leo Corbett met Elmer Deane, the situation really escalated. Now they could defraud the paper company on a truly magnificent scale. It was really quite easy. The warehouse had three main customers: the paper manufacturer; a machinery outfit that made snowplows, chain saws, etc.; and a television manufacturer. A freight car might arrive with goods from all three customers; but if the paper company is billed as if the car carried only *its* goods, then there is a lot extra to be pocketed. The amount rose quickly to $300,000 per year—one-third for Corbett, one-third for Deane, and one-third for the warehouse manager. (Of course incidentals like bribes had to be deducted.) Spurred on by his successful experience with this customer, Corbett set up a similar arrangement with his other large customers. Top management was not watching; what is $200,000 out of a $400 million business? And anyway, what does top management know about bills of lading and demurrage charges?

Deane was living high on the hog for a man with a $16,000 salary. He had a $60,000 home, a summer place, and three cars. He could afford it; Corbett was handing him $10,000 or $15,000 in cash at a time. (So casual was the operation that sometimes Deane was paid his cut by check.)

The recession comes along. The warehouse business, along with other businesses, was slow. Whereas he once received $10,000 to $15,000 at a time from Corbett, Deane was now getting merely $2,000 or $3,000. He was not geared to such a sharp decrease in income. He wished he had a warehouse of his own—someplace that was not subject to economic vicissitudes, that presented no overhead—and in which he would not have to split with two partners.

The wish was father to the thought and to the action. Deane began to "use" a new warehouse—far away, in Wyoming. He was storing goods there and the paper company was paying the bills. Only no goods were really being shipped there; indeed, there was no warehouse, only a mailing address. With this mailing address, fake stationery and bills of various kinds, and his years of experience, Deane had created the perfect tool—a phantom warehouse.

Of course, it could not last indefinitely; but it lasted for a long time. Finally the pinch made management more cost conscious, and they began to look a little more closely at some expenses that had been taken for granted.

We were called in. It did not take long to find out what was going on. Here in the records were bills that had been received, and paid, for shipments on Christmas and New Year's days, times when there obviously had been no goods received. Here was a payment, made in July, for work that was claimed to have been done the previous November. The bill went right through the system. When our representative asked the clerk why he had paid in July for services dating back nine months—without a shred of documentation —the clerk (who was not dishonest, only apathetic) replied in surprise, "Why it said right there on the paper to pay it."

It is often these workaday, unnoticed, unglamorous parts of a business that permit the thief greatest latitude. Here, in the "seams," he can ply his illegal trade without anyone knowing or understanding what he is doing.

Few of us are so blasé about air travel that we don't take a look at the captain as he walks through the cabin and try to assess his skill, resourcefulness, and dependability. Practically all captains have the looks to meet our expectations, and they have the ability, too.

Do you ever wonder what happens to that captain when he gets too old to fly jets? Well, flying is what he knows, so he is likely to stay in the airline business in one way or another. Some retired pilots use their

knowledge and contacts to build up a profitable business selling planes and spare parts to airlines all
over the world. This can be a pretty good vocation; and
it can be very profitable when the ex-captain is able
to sell equipment for ten times what he pays for it.
Unfortunately, this is what sometimes happens—at the
expense of the established airlines who used to be his
employers.

Here is what happens. A retired pilot drives to the
central warehouse of his old airline and drops in on the
girl in charge of stores. "Hey, Pete," she exclaims en-
thusiastically, "long time no see. What brings you
here?" Pete replies: "Nice to see you, Madge. You're
looking as sexy as ever. Got any radar outfits lying
around? I could use one. If you've got anything for
salvage. . . ." She purses her lips; "No units in salvage
category, Pete, but let me see what I can do."

Five minutes later the girl is back. She has taken a
complete radar set out of the active spare-part status,
separated it on the books into twelve pieces, and
marked them all "salvage." Pete writes a check of
$1,200 for an item that cost in excess of $30,000. Before
long the radar is on its way to a South American customer.

This kind of activity is particularly prevalent when
airlines are phasing out older planes and replacing them
with new ones. The opportunities for fraud are vast;
and the situation is difficult to control.

Safety, of itself, lies neither in being big nor being
small. The brand of business crime may vary according to size; but it does exist. Whatever the size of
the organization, vulnerability can be diminished only
by common-sense management that cuts both temptation and opportunity down to a minimum.

Let's take the Grimsley Organ Company. There are
few businesses more familylike than the organ business.

A youngster begins as a bench-boy and spends a lifetime making organs. Even those who leave the organ manufacturer stay in the field in some way or another, selling organs or servicing them. This is the business that they know.

The Grimsley Organ Company was particularly familylike. Workers who had left to go into selling or service were always welcome when they dropped around to buy parts or just to shoot the breeze. Employees were encouraged to play the organ—many in this business play quite well—and the employer would even permit them to borrow organs for special church or social affairs.

One young man had started with Grimsley when he was sixteen and had been with the company for ten years. He was a particularly gifted player, and his employer was proud to lend him the finest and most costly instruments to play concerts at the convention hall. Naturally, these instruments were always returned.

But it turned out that on certain other matters involving the young man, Grimsley was not so lucky. As a matter of fact, when our investigators caught up with him he confessed to stealing 130 different organs, with values running from $500 to $20,000. He and his friends were selling the instruments, at a discount, to the same dealers who handled Grimsley's output through legitimate channels. Moreover, this young man was only one among many. The Grimsley Company was being robbed, wholesale, by dozens of its "family" members, present and past.

At this point the reader can be pardoned for expressing a little skepticism. After all, a case of cosmetics or even a pneumatic tool is understandable, but how can a man steal even one organ, let alone 130? Actually it was quite simple. The Grimsley plant is three blocks long. Throughout, at the various workbenches, there are instruments in various stages of

work. There is always traffic around the loading dock
—not only completed instruments on their way to
dealers, but also loaned organs and organs that have
been sent in for servicing and are being returned to the
owners. The young man and his associates simply
backed up a truck and took the instruments away.

But wouldn't management miss something as big as
an organ? After all, the inventory was not in the hundreds of thousands. The answer lies in the control system. Grimsley organs were numbered consecutively as
they came off the line, and each unit was marked with
a metal plaque bearing the serial number, which was
then recorded in the company's books. The employee
who operated the punching machine that produced
the metal plaques was a key man in the theft operation; he simply made duplicate plaques upon request.
And as long as the consecutive numbering seemed to
be in order, no one asked any questions.

But the stealing of completed organs was not the
only way that Grimsley was being victimized. Workers
operated at benches, turning out individual components; they also developed the ability to construct
complete organs by themselves, and they gradually furnished their home workshops with the necessary equipment to do this. Thus, by judicious theft of needed
parts, it was not difficult for a Grimsley worker to
assemble a $10,000 instrument in his basement.

Former employees, beloved and welcomed with open
arms, were by no means slack in getting on the gravy
train. They walked in and out of the plant in perfect
freedom, often taking a part here and a part there. Ex-
members of the Grimsley "family" who had set themselves up in the business of servicing organs were able
to keep their overhead costs at a minimum by dropping
in on the friendly man who sold parts and buying
twenty parts for the price of one.

The unfortunate owners of the Grimsley Company

found to their great sorrow that the family approach does not necessarily develop loyalty. Indeed, the easy, paternal approach sometimes fosters theft of tremendous magnitude. And we find over and over that it is the ingrown, handicraft kind of operation that is particularly susceptible to this phenomenon.

The annual report of a chain of discount centers showed a substantial loss, which could be attributed only to inventory shrinkage. When we were called in, we focused first on one store and one manager. There were things going on at this store that were not in conformance with company policy. Management decided to let the manager go. At the time, he happened to be on vacation in Phoenix. He was called back and given the bad news. Surprisingly, the scene was not as difficult as had been anticipated. The manager accepted his dismissal with little comment.

The next move was to get the store in shape for the new manager to take over. The cash registers were checked, and the cash on hand balanced. Now, this store, like many stores, had a flexible system to take care of peak customer traffic. When the lines at the checkout counter became long, the manager would open up an extra cash register. Normally, receipts were accounted for every night. But the receipts from the extra register set up by this manager were treated differently. The manager accumulated the money taken in on peak days and put it in his safe. He used this money as a weekly reserve to cover shortages, and to balance out receipts on slow days so that he could "meet" his figures. This was against company policy; the controller knew about it, but closed his eyes.

When the safe in this particular store was opened, a bag of cash was found. Inside the bag was a note, signed by the ex-manager: "IOU $6,900." Of course there was an immediate hurry-up call to the manager to come into the office. He had been expecting the call, and he came in. The former employee was quite candid: "I was tipped off that something was in the wind before I left on vacation. You broke up my trip to Phoenix, made me come back at my expense with my wife and two kids. Well, I won't argue. I figure you owe me $6,900, so I took it. Why the hell should I sue you? You sue me."

After he left, his employers debated the big question: was this to be considered a criminal act, or a loan? Finally they decided upon a civil action to recover. Before the action went very far, the ex-manager died of a heart attack.

The casual approach may seem pleasant in the short run, but management's manifestation of the attitude that it does not take controls too seriously will inevitably engender lack of respect for those controls down the line.

Banks, of course, are prime targets. Every now and then we read about the trusted teller who over the years has embezzled hundreds of thousands of dollars. Fraud in banks involves a great deal of variety and ingenuity. Here's just one example.

This case involves a bank, a used-car dealer, and soldiers. The locale is a large army base, a depot for soldiers whose next stop is an overseas assignment. Near the gates of the base is "automobile row," a vista of used-car emporiums with chrome glistening and banners flying. None of these places is more gaudy than "Honest Harry's."

The local bank wanted to increase consumer product loans and started to solicit the automobile dealers, thinking this was a good avenue. The credit manager brought in Honest Harry as a customer.

Honest Harry offers the young soldier a deal he can hardly turn down: *No Down Payment* and a *Fine Car of Your Choice.* So the private, soon on his way overseas and in need of wheels for his off-post activities in the meantime, makes his way to Harry's. The soldier starts looking at the cheapest cars. But Harry steers Jimmy toward a late model Grand Prix. Jimmy never dreamed he could afford such a stupendous wagon. After all, he hasn't got a nickel. He hesitantly mentions this, and Harry laughs loudly. The used-car magnate points to the sign. "Doesn't that say no down payment? Would I say it if it wasn't true? Kid, don't worry about a thing. I know what you want—good wheels. And I want you to wheel *in style.* I know how it is—I was in your shoes once. You just leave everything to me."

Harry has Jimmy sign some papers. The cost of the car is $2,400; pretty high, but Jimmy isn't worried. If there is really not going to be any down payment, then Jimmy does not expect that there is going to be *any* payment. In a month he'll be overseas. They can take the crate back. Harry says, "Kid, I want you to write me a check for $500." Jimmy leaps from his chair—"I *told* you I didn't have any bank account." But Harry calms him down. "Who said anything about a bank account? I just want you to take *this* check"—Harry gives him a check issued by the Grand National Bank— "and make it out to me. Just part of the paperwork."

Jimmy makes out the check. Harry looks it over and says: "Fine. Now, I want you to take these papers over to the Continental People's Bank. Talk to Miss Arnold; she'll take care of everything." Jimmy shrugs; he is still a little doubtful, but those wheels are tempting.

Then Harry has one more thought . . . "Oh, kid. One more thing. You'll get a lot better service over there if they think you're something a little up the ranks from a buck private—that's the way they are. So I want you to just make a little change of clothes. . . ."

Harry leads the astonished Jimmy into a back room. Here are arrayed racks of officers' uniforms. While Jimmy gapes, Harry picks out a first lieutenant's outfit, saying, "I think these'll fit you nicely." Jimmy protests, but at last he goes along. He puts on the officer's uniform and goes to the bank to see Miss Arnold. And Jimmy's papers are processed in jig time. That evening he is behind the wheel of a car that was beyond his wildest dreams that morning.

The soldier is not the only one who is happy. Honest Harry is happy; he has sold a $1,500 car for $2,400 and gotten his money. The bank is happy; it has been enjoying an upsurge in auto loan business. The credit manager is happy; he gets $200 for every loan he approves. And Miss Arnold is happy; she gets $50 for "verification" of credit applications passed on to her by the credit manager—after which it is her job to destroy them.

Of course, the crunch comes for the bank when it begins to see the vast number of auto loans that are not being collected. The shortages amount to hundreds of thousands of dollars. Panic sets in. What has gone wrong?

What has gone wrong is that Honest Harry and his inamorata, Miss Arnold, and the credit manager have bilked the bank of a substantial chunk of its assets. When Harry sees the edifice beginning to crumble, he hotfoots it out of town leaving Miss Arnold and the credit manager to face the consequences, and the bank with the problem of a stack of uncollectable loans and a lot of cars scattered all over the countryside, many of them reduced to little more than junk by the enthusiastic G.I.'s who became part of Honest Harry's scheme.

5 WHY THEY BITE THE HAND
THAT FEEDS THEM

Why do employees defraud their employers? Greed for money is only one of the reasons. In this chapter we look inside the heads and hearts of some people you know.

Love of money is not the root of all evil. Though naturally a great deal of employee dishonesty is committed purely for the purpose of gain, there are other complicating factors that drive people to steal or destroy. The material gains may simply be a by-product; he undermines the business of his employer and violates his own self-image because of other compulsions.

A knowledge of some of these diverse motivations is essential to anyone involved in the detection and prevention of business crime. Some feel these underlying factors can be of use to any businessman who wants to protect himself from serious loss.

THE URGE TOWARD PUNISHMENT

Some manifestations of exposed business crime are so blatant, so palpable, that one is inclined to shake his head and ask, "How did he ever think he could get away with it?" Psychologists offer us one answer:

61

the individual does not want to get away with it; he wants to be caught. To the normal person this does not make much sense. And it seems to make even less sense when we add the observation that, while a certain kind of criminal wants to be caught, he does not realize that he wants to be caught. Dr. David Abrahamsen, in his book *Who Are the Guilty?* writes:

> . . . a man, when he commits a crime, is driven into it largely by unconscious forces. He may believe that he knows the motivations, but if he does, he knows usually the least important ones. The powerful motivations which are the actual motor behind the act are repressed and forgotten. Also, these motives are irrational. As a matter of fact, when we think of criminal behavior, we are again and again astounded to see how senseless and purposeless it frequently is.

This pattern—the need to be caught—is often seen more clearly among younger criminals. David Loth, in *Crime in the Suburbs*, comments on the seemingly senseless lawbreaking that we find increasingly among the children of the well-to-do:

> . . . in Edina, the wealthiest suburb of Minneapolis, the police have come to expect little groups of teenage shoplifters every autumn. Anticipating the wave of petty thefts, the juvenile officers are able to stop the teenagers before much harm is done. Apparently once most of the children who engage in these pastimes have won status by their crimes they revert to acceptable, or at least lawful behavior.

Attaining status among peers lies at the root of much teenage crime that is otherwise inexplicable; the youngster who is seeking peer approval surreptitiously filches a few items and then hurries out of the store to display his or her loot to the gang. But any store security official can testify that this is not the whole story.

Often we find something like the following: A store detective spots a boy, about fifteen, wandering aimlessly along the counters, fingering merchandise. The youth picks up a battery charger, peers at it closely, then clumsily sticks it in a side pocket. He moves on to a flashlight; the same thing happens. The boy glances sidewise; he cannot help but notice that he is being observed. Nevertheless, he rounds the corner into another department and pockets, with only a perfunctory effort at concealment, a pair of pinking shears. Chances are that he is only vaguely familiar with its use. The youth makes his way through the store, without any move toward the door, selecting diverse items—until he is apprehended.

He is asking to be caught. And child psychologists, policemen, and juvenile authorities in suburban areas —who know this pattern only too well—tell us that the culprit is asking for more than just to be caught. He is *crying for help*. His school, his family, the world are out of joint for him; by being caught he not only attracts the attention he is seeking, but brings about a miniature cataclysm in the midst of which he can throw up his hands and say: "Well, they've got me. Nothing more I can do. Now it's up to them."

A similar lemming-like urge toward detection and disaster can be found in the worker who steals even when he has every reason to know that he is suspected and that the risk of punishment is now a certainty. Moreover, whether this individual is stealing money, merchandise, or equipment, it is usually a reasonable assumption that he does not need the loot, has little use for it, and is only stealing because he needs to commit a crime—and get caught.

Strangely enough, people who rob an employer blatantly, with only the most perfunctory effort at concealment, often manage to go on doing it for a surprisingly long time. It is not that they go unobserved; it would be hard not to observe them. But observation does not mean detection; and sometimes the very senselessness and audacity of business crime serves to blind employers, supervisors, and colleagues to the fact that it is going on. The man who boldly walks out the gate, openly carrying a piece of test equipment, is more likely to get by than the man who attempts to hide a similar piece of equipment under his windbreaker. The secretary who opens up the cash box and takes out money in full view is less apt to be seized than her working sister who does the same thing when she thinks nobody is looking. Sometimes, against a great deal of weighty evidence, we assume that people are rational, even though they may be dishonest. And so the combination of dishonesty and irrationality sets up a shield of invisibility as complete as that effected by the Tarnhelm in the legend of the Ring of the Nibelungs.

SPITE AND SABOTAGE

A man stands in a steaming, reeking telephone booth located in the waiting room of a bus terminal. He is trying to make an important long-distance call. Peering desperately at the faint numerals, with little help from the feeble rays cast by a tiny electric bulb, he dials the number, and then obediently deposits the requested amount of change in the slot. Nothing happens; no ring, no busy signal; nothing. He hangs up, then removes the handpiece again and jiggles the hook. There is no welcome jingle. He does not get his money back. And it was all the change that he had.

Now this man knows what he is supposed to do. He is supposed to obtain another dime and report his loss to the operator, who will take his name and address. Eventually he will receive in the mail a chit for the amount of change that the coin telephone refused to regurgitate for him. As we say, the man knows what is required in this situation. But does he do it? No. He commences to bang the instrument with the flat of his hand, moderately at first, and then with increasing violence, until finally he is hammering upon the device with unmerciful ferocity. This action yielding no satisfaction, he yanks savagely at the handset until the phone parts from its moorings; then he stalks away from the shambles.

And we onlookers, citizens who pretend to probity and civilized behavior, what do we do? Do we properly condemn this miscreant? Do we point the finger of scorn and anathema at him for his unlawful and brazen act? No. We smile and applaud. We understand how he feels.

The man banging on the telephone coin box is making his pointed, if ineffectual, protest against the world of increasingly gigantic and impersonal institutions. There is a good deal of this today; but it is not an altogether new phenomenon. In England, at the beginning of the nineteenth century, machine-made goods began to replace handicrafts. Many people lost their livelihood; but beyond the economic factor, there was at first a smoldering, and then blazing resentment toward technology as an agent of dehumanization. Bands of masked men—called "Luddites" after their mythical leader General Ludd—rose in Nottingham and the neighboring districts to riot and destroy factories and machines. The rebellion against technology spread into a number of counties, and was put down only after shootings, hangings, and a wholesale shedding of blood. And the Luddite feeling persisted for generations.

In an unorganized, uncentralized fashion we are seeing the spread of a new Luddite rebellion. People feel that their lives are being run by machines; and they don't like it. It is the ultimate depersonalization. Much of the resentment focuses on the computer, as human beings express their protest at what they conceive to be "folding, spindling, and mutilation." But there is plenty of animus left over for other machines—and for organizations that seem increasingly faceless and machinelike in their dealings with people.

The businessman who protests against such giants as the telephone company and the commuter railroad, and indeed, who has done his share of coin box banging, is often amazed to learn that his *own* organization is considered to be a faceless monolith by some of those who work in it. On too many occasions the businessman learns this unpleasant fact the hard way when a worker commits a grandiose act of destructive dishonesty or sabotage just because he has been driven beyond reasonable limits by his frustration. Even the businessman who prides himself on knowing every face and name may find, to his dismay, that his friendliness has not acted as a protective talisman against spiteful retaliation.

Any company, large or small, can unwittingly become a target for sabotage. Jones, the assistant head of the records department at the headquarters of Essential Metals, Inc., turned down many job offers over the years because he thought that when his boss retired he would succeed him, with a handsome increase in salary. The boss's day of retirement came, along with several other developments. Essential Metals had suffered some reverses which impelled management to look into ways of reducing operating costs. And, one step was the consolidation of the records department with another department. When he was told that he would be assistant to the head of the combined departments, it was shattering enough. Worse, he learned that he would be working for a woman. On the surface he took this disappointment unemotionally but, as we learned later, inside he was seething with rage.

The disappointed man secretively embarked on a series of incidents to discredit the woman and to scare her out of the job. Records were misplaced or destroyed. Other documents were drenched in red ink obliterating the figures. Data prepared for the computers was tampered with, resulting in wholesale rejections by the machines. False bomb scares and the arrival of the police bomb squad became a frequent and unsettling occurrence. One afternoon a fire suddenly broke out in the ventilator over her head and, finally, to top it off, he put sleeping pills in her morning coffee.

Jones has long since gone from Essential Metals but the company has not yet recovered from the havoc he wrought.

We see resentment in the clerk who feels her extra efforts are not appreciated. Nora Thorp was requested to come in early because the auditors were expected momentarily. She came in at 8:00 o'clock instead of 9:00, gave up her coffee break, and skipped her lunch. At 3:00 o'clock, instead of thanking her, the office manager said, "Now, you have to help Mary Brown." She protested: "Mary Brown! I haven't spoken to her in four years. She's a flirt; always on the phone with personal calls; never comes back from lunch on time. This is the thanks I get." Later she admits that she

tore up Mary Brown's backlog of paperwork consisting of $16,000 worth of accounts receivable documents
and flushed the fragments down the toilet.

We see this same rebellion in the warehouse clerk
who was in charge of bringing reserve stock to the
lines. When the lines could not absorb it all he took
the surplus back to his own stock area, where he had
set up over fifty small cubicles for which he developed
a locater system and from which he pulled the items
again when he needed them. This gave him a feeling of
importance. He wanted a desk and chair to support his
ego. He was repeatedly told that the desk and chair
were on order but they never materialized. So he built
a desk out of wooden crates and improvised to make
it attractive. For a chair, as he later told us, he had
been appropriating chairs from other employees' desks.
However, as soon as they were missed they would be
taken away from him. His frustration became so great
that one night he returned to the plant, threw flam-
mable fluid on the floor, ignited it, and burned a brand
new warehouse to the ground.

Such spiteful hatred of an organization goes hand
in hand, the psychologists tell us, with a feeling of guilt
and inadequacy. Dr. Ernest Jones, the pioneer psychoanalyst and author of the definitive biography of Freud,
observes: "Hatred for someone implies that the other
person, through his cruelty or unkindness, is the cause
of one's sufferings, that the latter are not self-imposed
or in any way one's own fault. All the responsibility for
the misery produced by unconscious guilt is thus dis-
placed on to the other." It is easy to attribute one's
troubles to an institution, particularly when that institution is the one for which you work.

So some people steal and destroy just for the satisfaction of getting back at the system that has, in their

view, caused all their difficulties. Motivation and rationale fit together nicely; the impulse wells up from the almost universal drive to attack the organization.

It is not just the obvious malcontent who engages in spiteful retaliation against his employer. Over and over, businessmen are shocked to find that the smiling, loyal worker who has been with the firm for many years has been engaged in systematic looting over a considerable period. Indeed, it may well be that the hostility that results in such destruction is more likely to build up behind the smiling mask than behind the disgruntled face from which gripes are continually being emitted.

STATUS

"I would never want to go back to that. I'd steal first," you will hear a man say. The thought, in more or less that form, comes into the minds of a good many people. What is the *that* to which it would be so unbearable to return? It could be a state of abject poverty; but more often the reference is to a previously experienced situation in which the individual's status was not so high as it is now.

Status is a tremendously powerful motivator. And in our society status is thoroughly entwined with success —specifically, success in business that maintains a high income, attractive home, several cars, and conspicuously expensive leisure activities, and that offers the opportunity to "provide the best for the children."

Children are important in any discussion of status. A man who has clawed his way to the top scarcely rationalizes his struggle in terms of the satisfactions he has drawn from it; rather, he has "done it for the family." In *Crestwood Heights*, a sociological study of the culture of suburban life, authors John R. Seeley, R. Alexander Sim, and Elizabeth W. Loosley observe:

> Status, in Crestwood Heights, is somewhat like a commodity—similar to money, but perhaps more enduring. The Crestwooder, faced by annual income tax and periodic death duties, rarely thinks of money in terms of inherited wealth; he acquires it by his own efforts . . . the child, in his turn, will "earn his own way" as an adult as far as money is concerned. Status, however, is seen in a somewhat different light. It must be won, like money, but it can more readily be conferred. Family status, handed on to the children, is a real and tangible asset.

In a real sense, the ability to acquire status and pass it on to the children has come to be the acid test of achievement in our society. And when a high-achieving man finds his transferable status in jeopardy, he may go to great extremes to keep it from slipping away.

Of course, the precarious nature of status is rarely recognized by the individual who has amassed a goodly amount of it—or at least he doesn't think about its possible loss when things are going well. William H. Whyte, Jr., in *The Organization Man* described one aspect of his subject's point of view:

> Depression? They don't even think about it. If they are pressed into giving an opinion on the matter, their explanations would suggest that America has at last found something very close to the secret of perpetual motion. And the gears, they believe, can no longer be reversed. . . . "The government would certainly see to it that a depression would not take place." In the unlikely event one did take place, some add, it wouldn't hurt them personally. Whatever their occupation, almost all organiza-

tion people feel their particular job is depression-proof.

Well, it has been amply demonstrated that America has not found the secret of perpetual motion. We may not use the word "depression"—but we have seen the economic gears slip, if not actually go into reverse. And many people have felt the sands of status shifting beneath their feet.

For some it is too much. They give up. Robert S. Gallagher has written a book, *If I Had It To Do Over Again,* about America's adult dropouts—the people who just disappear. Gallagher says:

> For decades they obeyed the rules and regulations trying, with varying degrees of success, to do what they felt was expected of them. Initially their inculcated expectations were high and gilded with bright promise. They did what they were told, and told themselves that it would all work out all right in the end. But as time passed, their optimism gave way to despair, their identity was challenged, their confidence badly crippled. At this anxious moment —their departure point—these men and women, who are so much like the rest of us, faced the modern dilemma of continuing to exist with a sense of helplessness in an indifferent world. . . . Suddenly they were gone.

But others do not give up. They fight with every resource at their disposal, fair or foul. There is an analogy in competitive sports. The late Vince Lombardi achieved a place near the zenith of the American pantheon because he was a football coach to whom "winning is not everything; it's the *only* thing." Robert K. Merton, writing in *Social Theory and Social Structure* (reprinted in *Delinquency, Crime, and Social Process,*

Cressey and Ward), talks about the processes that result in "anomie," a state of society in which normative standards of belief or conduct are weak or lacking:

> Thus, in competitive athletics, when the aim of victory is shorn of its institutional trappings and success becomes construed as "winning the game" rather than "winning under the rules of the game," a premium is implicitly set upon the use of illegitimate but technically efficient means . . . the emphasis on the goal has so attenuated the satisfactions derived from sheer participation in the competitive activity that only a successful outcome provides gratification.

Winning is the only thing. And in this philosophy, sports mirrors our values as we apply them to the larger world.

Let's take the case of a division manager of an organization. Under today's results-oriented management approach, he has a high degree of autonomy. Those in the top echelons expect him to deliver the goods; how he does it is his business. Times become hard; it is more difficult to deliver the expected results than it used to be. The manager's bonuses dwindle. Furthermore, there are ominous rumblings from on high. No one comes right out and says it, but there is an undeniable hint that if results are not forthcoming somebody else will be brought in.

Now, we are talking about a man who has made watching the Sunday afternoon football games a kind of religion. And this man needs more than just the stimulation of observing skillful players execute their patterns. He wants *his* team to *win*. And if it happens that a massive defensive end from *his* team smashes into the opposing quarterback after the whistle has blown, and the opposing quarterback does not get up, he doesn't draw back from the television set in horror. He grins and applauds. *That* is the way to win.

This same man's employer is threatening his job— and not just his job, but his status, which comprises the house, the education he is giving his children, the cabin cruiser moored down at the shore, and incidentally, the enormous color set on which he watches the games. Is it reasonable to expect that this division manager will scrupulously observe all of the accepted codes of moral behavior under the pressure of the threatened deprivation? Certainly not. He will fight to win. He will, if necessary, begin to juggle figures and inventories so that he can deliver the results that the head office demands. Or, if he sees his grip upon his status slipping away, he will get the money to maintain that status by stealing it from the company. The question is not whether it is right or wrong; the question is, how skillfully can he do it, and how long can he get away with it? When status is the prize, the "game ethic" comes into play with a vengeance.

Management must recognize that status is a double-edged weapon. The need to achieve drives men on, and makes them perform prodigies that result in profit for the organization. But the threat of losing status will drive a man to bold and desperate means. Many companies have been the losers in this game.

THE SELF-EFFACING EGOTIST

In most organizations there is at least one of a type whom we might call the company altruist. This is the good-hearted individual. The altruist arranges the party and passes the hat when an employee is leaving. The

organization's good works—help for the blind, the re-
tarded, the poor—usually involve the altruist and wind
up being run by him.

This mild-mannered, self-effacing person was never
heard to tear anyone down. A pleasure to have around
and a credit to any company. Other workers, who secretly admit to their occasional base emotions, marvel
at the saintliness of the altruist. It is not unusual to hear
the president or board chairman say to a visitor: "Now,
you take old Sam, down in the mail room. Sam is our
pride and joy. Whenever one of our kids gets in trouble,
we send him to Sam—and he takes over. He has
straightened out more boys . . . and put in plenty of
his own time to do it, too. . . ."

Now and then this good, mild-mannered employee
can go wrong; he can become an industrial thief. And
this motivation may be based firmly upon his big heart.
When this happens, it is a particularly difficult thing
to rationalize. For one thing, the altruist who is stealing
is not easily detected; not only is he not suspected, he
is not even thought of when security measures are contemplated. No one who is *that* generous and *that* loyal
could possibly be dishonest. Thus, when the revelation
comes, the shock is immense; and the unfortunate tendency is to conclude that *nobody* is honest and to institute rigorous measures that do not stop theft but *do*
turn employees off.

The dishonest altruist is an exception; but he is not as
rare a bird as many businessmen would like to think.
Here is a case of a misguided do-gooder from our files.

A manufacturing company in New York employs
hundreds of assembly-line workers, many of them from
the Caribbean, hired right off the plane. These people,
by and large, are good workers, but language and cultural differences create problems. For example, workers
did not understand the time clock system; they would

walk around with their cards in their pockets, or leave them unclocked in the rack. At the end of the week Dan Spofford, the plant manager, often had to write in the time or make a change on the card so that his people could be paid. Spofford had arranged with the paymaster for this procedure. He did not mind; he had developed a great affection for these people.

Even with this arrangement, however, the workers often ran out of money. They would find themselves unable to pay their bills in the company cafeteria. Spofford was continually reaching into his own pocket for a couple of dollars here and there to tide them over. But still the cafeteria manager complained that "these people are beating me out of money."

"All right," Dan Spofford finally said, "I don't want to lose the help, and anyway these are nice folks. Give them credit. When they get their paychecks I'll hold them. I'll make sure they cash them and I'll see that you get paid." This arrangement worked all right; but Dan Spofford discovered a curious thing. Sometimes the workers disappeared without claiming their last paychecks; so there he was, stuck with the uncashed checks. The cafeteria manager had to get what was owed him, so what could be more logical than for Spofford to endorse the checks and pay what was owed? After all, if the bills were not paid, the cafeteria manager would crack down on credit for all of the workers.

There was unclaimed money left over; and gradually Spofford came to think of it as his. Not, of course, that he would use it for himself, but rather to help out the workers. It was at this point that Dan Spofford's affection for his workers started to become a bit selective. No longer did he embrace *all* of the newly arrived workers—only those who were "good" workers. Naturally there were a few bad apples in the barrel;

why should they spoil it for their hard-working brothers? So Spofford became a little tougher. He began to fire the really unproductive employees. It was normal procedure with one little difference. Spofford would keep the time cards of the fired workers in the rack for two or three additional weeks. What did the paymaster know? All the names—Perez, Santos, García—sounded alike anyway. So the manager was able to obtain more money to continue his growing program of kindness to the workers he loved.

Ultimately Spofford was caught. He protested that he had not taken the money for himself, but to help his friends. No matter; he was fired, and he lost twenty-three years' participation in the pension plan and $19,000 in profit-sharing.

We have come upon numerous other instances of altruism run wild. The underlying motives seem to be rooted in the misguided unselfishness of the individual who commits the acts. But in our view, and that of psychologists who have closely observed such phenomena, it is erroneous to suppose that people who steal from the company to help others are devoid of ego. On the contrary, we find that, hidden beneath the surface veneer of meekness and self-effacement, there is often a complex of self-esteem that has grown to enormous proportions. Self-conferred nobility can lead to something approaching a "superman" mentality that exempts one from the rules that govern ordinary mortals.

The German philosopher Friedrich Nietzsche might have been describing the moral platform from which the altruistic thief projects his attitude when he wrote:

> The noble type of man regards *himself* as a determiner of values; he does not require to be approved of; he passes the judgment: "What is injurious to me is injurious in itself"; he knows that it is he him-

self only who confers honor on things; he is a creator of values. . . . At the risk of displeasing innocent ears, I submit that egoism belongs to the essence of a noble soul, I mean the unalterable belief that to such a being as "we," other beings must naturally be in subjection, and have to sacrifice themselves.

Driven by a conviction of nobility of motive and self, such an individual makes his own rules. The money, material, and equipment of the employer are his to do with what he wishes, because he is not appropriating another's possession for ignoble purposes. The twisted, self-effacing altruist, although he has a simplistic view of the world, its morality, and his relationship to it, is by no means a naive or maladroit thief. On the contrary, his conviction that he is right, and better than others who are wrong, impels him to exert every resource of wiliness and camouflage to pursue his ends in the interests of a higher morality. Thus he is a doubly dangerous adversary: his mien averts suspicion, and his inner egotism forces him to extremes of complexity in his defalcations.

LOVE

"Amor vincit omnia," sang the poet Virgil; and we see evidence every day that these words are true. For some people, love *does* conquer all—conventional morality, family attachments, business ethics, and common sense. Here we use the term "love" in rather a broad sense, to comprehend the multitude of sexual entanglements into which men and women involve themselves, and for the maintenance of which they are driven to do almost anything, including stealing.

Obviously the professional concerned with business security is neither a crusader nor a reformer. But he cannot avoid seeing, over and over, the overpowering effect that sex can have upon an ostensibly upright, intelligent, reliable individual in business. A person "becomes involved"; he may maintain his involvement on a superficial level, but even this common enough practice has its dimensions in profit-and-loss figures.

Recently an audiovisual expert who had just formed his own company was negotiating with a firm for the production of a training film. Everything seemed to be set. The firm's training director liked his work and there was no question that he could do a satisfactory job. Nor was there any question about the fee; but there was some mysterious, oblique conversation about how that fee was to be stated—and this baffled the audiovisual man. Finally the training director came out with it: "The point is this: you will add $1,500 to your bill, and this comes back under the table—$500 for the division manager, $500 for the advertising manager, $500 for me." All three company officials were playing around with women. This requires money, and so every opportunity had to be taken to generate cash in ways that could not be detected by either the organization or the wife at home.

Here at the superficial level we find a kind of casual morality that might be shrugged off with, "It's all right to play around; who doesn't? The big thing is not to get caught." Since a man who is "playing around" needs to go first class, there is a constant demand for cash, and it is perfectly okay to rob the company to get it. Just do it so that no explanations have to be made. At this level there is no feeling of guilt; the moral approach to sexual and financial ethics is the same.

But when the involvement becomes intense and personal, guilt makes its appearance. One heartbreaking case was that of a middle-aged, successful manager with a wife and a growing family. His latent homosexuality burst through, and he fell in love with an unscrupulous young man and defrauded his employer of really awesome amounts of money for the benefit of his lover. In this case the cargo of tragedy and guilt was immense: but there is, of course, no paucity of guilty feelings in a conventional illicit relationship.

When a man feels that he is sinning against and hurting those who love him, he becomes a kind of outlaw. Other laws and regulations pale into insignificance beside the great wrong which he knows he is committing, but from which he cannot withdraw. This man becomes highly vulnerable; if he must steal from the company in order to maintain his relationship or to conceal his transgression, he will do so. This is why sex and business theft so often seem to go hand in hand.

The situation is dangerous enough when the individual's extramarital activity takes place off the business premises. But when such a relationship arises between people working in the same firm, the dangers are compounded. Their mutual attraction binds them together against the world; and the world that seems to threaten them most immediately—and thus must be struck back against—is the business world within which they work. It may begin with just the exchange of privileged information—the sales manager telling the secretary, over an intimate cocktail, about the top-secret marketing plan. It may progress to the granting of favors—the woman in the bookkeeping department speeding through the paperwork of her lover in the purchasing department to help him look good. The likely progress of such a necessarily clandestine alliance is then to theft—at first almost imperceptible, then on to serious larceny.

Business crime that is deeply involved with, and caused by, passion is perhaps the most poignant in its consequences. When it is finally uncovered, the culprits' whole lives totter and collapse. Worse, in the moment of exposure the lovers often turn upon each other; and what began, perhaps, with a touching mutual exchange of sympathy and understanding ends in an acrid atmosphere of bitterness and recrimination. There are few spectacles that are more devastating.

6 SCHOOL FOR DISHONESTY

The worker who is stealing from your company at this moment may have gotten his impetus from the job. Some businessmen unwittingly turn their employees into thieves. Here is how it happens.

Recent studies reveal that certain dynamics that are built into the employment situation are the largest contributing factors in the turn toward dishonesty. These factors can be identified and discussed; but first it might be well to make some observations on a question we are often asked: "How can people go to church and believe in honesty and ethics, and *still* steal from their employers?" The question, it is hardly necessary to add, is asked by people who are not enmeshed in fraud, or have not yet become seriously dishonest, or at least have not been caught.

It's an important question. The business thieves who operate on the grandest scale are often pillars of the community and models of righteousness. Naturally, these are the people who are invested with the greatest trust and consequently have the greatest opportunity to steal. And they can't all be cynical pretenders, who deliberately hide behind the mask of respectability.

No. What we find, when we uncover major theft, are troubled people—people who would like to think of themselves as decent, but who have permitted themselves to wade deeper and deeper into a morass. And the will-o'-the-wisp that has led them on involves an elaborate process of rationalization.

People *are* somehow able to justify dishonesty within their minds, and to make it consistent with the self-image that they would like to maintain. This intellectual capacity to reconcile conflicting elements is the subject of an intriguing, still-debated but growingly accepted theory developed by the distinguished psychologist Leon Festinger. Festinger's formulation addresses itself to what he calls the phenomenon of *cognitive dissonance*. Simply put, the theory operates this way: the mind, when confronted with two sets of facts which create an uncomfortable psychological imbalance, *adjusts these facts to make them more harmonious . . . and thus reduce the "dissonance."*

In a typical experiment in cognitive dissonance, as reported in *Interpersonal*, the letter of management psychology, teenage girls were asked to rate twelve hit records in order of their preference. After the girls had made up their lists, the researchers went through the individual selections and told each subject that she would receive as a gift two of the records she had listed. The gifts were *not* the records *most* preferred; typically they would be sixth and ninth on a given list. After the awarding of the gifts, the girls were again asked to list their favorite records in order of preference. *And this time they valued the gift records much higher*. Similar experiments have been conducted frequently, using different subject matter and different subjects.

What had the girls done? The reception of the gift records set up a dissonance. The girls had originally valued other records higher, but that was before they knew they were to receive the less-preferred ones. How could they resolve this? By making a mental shift that enabled them to rate more highly that which they now possessed. It is said that the grass in the other fellow's back yard always looks greener; this experiment tends to show that through some cerebral evolutions we can brighten the greenness of our own premises.

This process of cognitive dissonance is also what leads to the following situation, with which many managers are familiar. Manager John Doe has a bright, promising young man, Bill Brown, in his department. A more responsible job opens up; but Doe decides that Brown is not quite ready for it. Doe hopes ardently that the young man will stay; he urges him to. But Bill Brown leaves, quickly getting a job with another firm.

There is a dissonance in John Doe's mind. He still thinks he did the right thing, and yet—maybe if he had known that he would lose such a potentially gifted worker as Brown he wouldn't have done it. And maybe he didn't read the situation right; maybe he did the wrong thing.

It gnaws at him—for a while. And then an odd thing happens. Bill Brown begins to look in retrospect not as good as he looked when he was around. And this counter-feeling grows until Doe is able to say things like: "Oh, he was a pretty bright young man in some aspects of the job. But he was immature; not much good at detail; rubbed people the wrong way. It's best that he left; he never would have worked out with us." This is how the manager resolves his dissonance about this episode.

The same factor, psychologists tell us, operates to urge people to follow avidly the advertising for an automobile *that they have just bought*. They still have doubts—dissonances. So they are helping themselves to reduce the conflict by continuing to rationalize that they got the best deal.

Our experience makes it evident that a dynamic much like Festinger's cognitive dissonance operates to enable an individual to justify stealing from his employer. On the one hand there is his urge to see himself as honest, straightforward, the possessor of the virtues that we have been taught from childhood to admire. The impulse to see ourselves as good people and to value ourselves highly is, psychologists have learned, a very strong impulse indeed. Into conflict with this desire comes a discordant set of facts. These involve the undeniable realization that the faking of an expense account, or the appropriation of an occasional item from stock, or the acceptance of favors from a supplier, would *not* be approved by management if the details became known. The action is dishonest; or at least the concealing of it is dishonest. A dissonance is set up, and the individual must resolve it some way. Of course he could stop doing dishonest things, but frequently his mind can find another route off the horns of the dilemma.

He rationalizes. As the alcoholic tells himself, "One won't hurt me; I can take it or leave it alone," so the business thief in the early stages finds an explanation for what he is doing. The explanation would probably not satisfy an outsider; but his debate is with himself, and he mounts a compelling enough argument in favor of dishonesty to quell the dissonances in his psyche.

And now a vital point. The management of his company may be making it *supremely easy for him to do this.*

Here are two examples of how it happens. Charles Black has, in a short time, established himself as one of the company's leading salesmen. Black is able to sell tough accounts through persuasive logic, attention to detail, and superb organization. The firm moves him into an executive job in the home office, and top management has high hopes that Black will keep on moving up the ladder.

Black's boss, Edwin Samson, does not baby his new subordinate. After a couple of days of orientation, he hands him a rough assignment: the complete rethinking and reorganization of the company's merchandising approach. The deadline for completion of the project is tight and the chances of success are by no means high. But Black finishes on time, and brings in a superb piece of work.

Now Samson wonders how he can reward this extraordinary effort. This bright new talent will be avidly sought by competitors, and Samson wants to bind him to the company. But he can't raise Black's salary; it has just been raised. He can't legitimately give him vacation time; the company policy is quite clear on that. So, Samson says: "Charlie, you've got to be tired out after all you've been doing. And Marian hasn't been seeing much of you these past few weeks. Why don't you and she just take off for a week—Miami Beach, if you like. Do you both good."

Black is appreciative of the thought; but there is the time, the expenses, the other things on the job that must be done. Samson has thought of all this. "Don't worry about it. We'll call it business. There must be a convention or some damn thing or other any place you go. I'll cover for you; and I'll pick up the tab for the whole thing. You've earned it."

Here is another case.

Peter Silas runs the luggage department in a large department store branch. It's tough to get intelligent, reliable sales clerks, and that's why Silas is delighted when the Personnel Department turns up Mrs. Purcell.

Mrs. Purcell is in her forties. Her children are grown, she has time on her hands, she'd like to do something and earn some money. She goes to work selling luggage, and Silas knows right from the first day that he has come into possession of a treasure. Mrs. Purcell is careful, capable, articulate, and very good with the customers.

The manager wants to do everything possible to keep this star performer around. About six weeks after she is hired, he is chatting with Mrs. Purcell. "I like working here very much," she says. "I like handling the fine goods, and talking with people about their travel needs. Of course, it's a little frustrating sometimes . . ." Silas perks up his ears. "Frustrating? How?"

Well, it seems that Mrs. Purcell's son will be going away to school. She would love to make him a present of this particular suitcase—a Louis Vuitton, the top of the line. "But even with my employee discount, it's too rich for my blood, Mr. Silas."

It has never crossed her mind that Mr. Silas could do something to bring the prized piece of luggage within her reach. But it crosses Silas's mind—and he acts. "Hmm . . . This case here, huh? It's a very nice piece. Let's see . . ." Silas does something that Mrs. Purcell cannot quite make out. And suddenly the metal nameplate on the case is askew. "Look at that," says Peter Silas. "Damaged merchandise. Now we'll have to let it go to you for half price—if you want it. Of course that tag will be easy to fix. I can show you how."

Mrs. Purcell learns fast, as her manager noticed. Two weeks later she is puzzling over another gift problem—a birthday present for her aunt. But she doesn't puzzle for long. She picks up an overnight case. There is a bobby pin in her hand. And a few minutes later the sales clerk is at the adjustment counter. "A customer brought this back. You see, there's a slight scratch on it here. Hardly noticeable, but I guess she's just fussy." The overnight case is marked down. Mrs. Purcell buys it for half price. And she is on her way.

In each case the boss has provided the subordinate with a ready-made rationalization for dishonesty. They don't expect that the subordinate will go on to bigger and worse things, but that part is out of the manager's control. Such a course, put in motion, rarely stops where the boss would like it to stop.

Why should managers do such things? For a number of reasons, some conscious and some unconscious.

Capable workers are scarce. We all know that. Nowadays when a manager loses a promising employee, the higher echelon wants to know why, so bosses are highly motivated to keep good people. They work hard to improve their "human relations." They think that all it takes is to talk nicely to employees and give them breaks. And to give a *really* good break to an employee, you may have to cut some corners. But this is done in a good cause. Management approves. So what can be wrong with it?

Another reason: most people who arrive at responsible management levels are nice people. They are not ogres. They like to be liked. But they run afoul of a reality of business life: often the boss is *not* loved— not because of any personal failing, but just because he is the boss. So a certain kind of executive will try to *buy* affection from his subordinates by condoning and even encouraging circumvention of the regulations. Nothing serious, of course; just a little something here and there to show that the boss is a human being . . . "Mr. Nice Guy."

In a way the power to do this is regarded as one of the privileges of rank . . . "It's my department; I can do what I like. If I want to give somebody a break, for a good cause, what's wrong with that?" So new employees are given an introduction to their work that spells out an easily readable message: you don't always have to obey the rules.

Managers sit at seminars and wonder aloud, across the conference table, at the decline in morality that has led so many employees into dishonesty. *These managers themselves are the seducers.*

And what gives this seduction its truly insidious quality is the fact that it is carried on, not with evil intent, but often from the most altruistic of motives. But the manager thinks little about the ultimate consequences, or how the example he is setting can easily lead to outright fraud. So by suggestion and example, he sets a tone of indifference toward scrupulous honesty, or at least he tacitly indicates that it is all right to be selective about honesty. Juggling the books, taking money from the till—these things you must not do. But taking some unauthorized time off, making off with an occasional piece of company property—these things are all right "within reason." Of course each individual becomes free to determine the limits of "reason." There is no fixed point at which the process may be designated as getting out of hand.

What makes all of this possible—the inadvertent seduction and the eager continuation into broader areas of dishonesty—is that increasingly the employing organization can be viewed as an impersonal abstraction. The employee sees the entity that pays his salary not as a person or a group of human beings, but as words or numbers on paper. C. Wright Mills, in his influential study, *White Collar*, comments on the phenomenon:

> From the executive's suite to the factory yard, the paper webwork is spun; a thousand rules you never made and don't know about are applied to you by a thousand people you have not met and never will. The office is the Unseen Hand become visible as a row of clerks and a set of IBM equipment, a pool of Dictaphone transcribers, and sixty

receptionists confronting the elevators, one above the other, on each floor.

Mills, to be sure, was writing about the corporate giant. There is a tendency for the smaller businessman or store owner to look at such formulations smugly and console himself with the thought that "My operation is not like that; I know all my people, etc." This is a dangerous delusion. As the methods of the giants have become accessible to the smaller enterprise; as mechanization, electronification, and big-company management concepts have seeped downward—there has been an increasing depersonalization of all business, large and small.

The company becomes an abstraction; and it is more easily justifiable to cheat an abstraction. When you unexpectedly get back more change in the telephone slot than you are entitled to, you are taking it from the telephone company, not from the operator or from any identifiable individual. And as the "company" becomes more remote, its policies become less real as guidelines to appropriate behavior. "Rules were made to be broken" was never more truly said than of company or store policy. The policy is something for the manager to "play against" as he cements relationships, wins friends, and (in his mind) binds good people to the organization. The policy is something for the subordinate to match his wits against if he feels the desire for a little extra money, a tool, or an attractive piece of merchandise.

As if those disadvantages were not enough, many organizations place an unbearable strain upon their policy structure by so overdetailing policy that serious limitations are imposed upon people who are just trying to do their jobs. Restrictive policies are usually not intended merely to eliminate fraud. The general aim is, more often than not, cost-cutting. But rigidity of policy can provide another incentive for managers, and in turn for their subordinates, to practice evasion and ultimate dishonesty. Firmness must not be allowed to become rigidity. The "taut ship" is desirable; the ship that is overencumbered will not perform well.

For example, a good many firms attempt to limit waste by limiting financial discretion down the organizational line. The power to approve expenditures of any significance is jealously guarded. This provides the illusion that money will be spent responsibly, and that only a few members of top management will have the final word in disbursements of any size. But what actually happens?

Let's take the advertising department of a manufacturing company. This operation is involved in creating numerous pieces of literature: catalogs, display photos, price lists, mailing pieces; new product brochures, and the like. The advertising manager has just hired a new assistant, and one of the first things that the new man hears is, "All expenditures of $500 or more have to be approved by the executive vice-president."

The assistant is bemused. He knows that many bills for printing, photography, and free-lance work run into figures far above $500. He asks: "Can I always get to see him? Sometimes these things have to be done in a hurry. If I have to sit around waiting for approval . . ." The advertising manager shakes his head, smiling. "Don't be a damn fool. What I just told you is what it says in the book. If we went by the book, we would never get anything out. The first thing you will have to learn is how to get suppliers to break up the invoices so that we don't need to get authorization." And the assistant quickly learns from a master who has developed a workable system for getting around the policy requirement.

Here we have responsible men devising ways to circumvent regulations. They are not doing it to cheat the company—at least not at the beginning. They are doing it because they would never get anything done if they meticulously followed the rules in the book. And they are being judged on results; pleading to management that the policy was too restrictive will not save them if they do not get the job done. So, in a limited way, these individuals are making the system workable by ignoring policy.

Policy is violated on a selective basis so that business can be done better (and, incidentally, this may well be happening with the knowledge of top management). But the criteria for selection of rules to be broken broaden and, almost imperceptibly, the process can slip into a situation in which employees and suppliers conspire to enrich themselves at the expense of the company. Here, indeed, is seduction that begins with the best of motives. And here management encourages the process by apathy and by the promulgation of unworkable policies.

7 HOW PRESSURE FOR
RESULTS CREATES OPPORTUNISTS

In our relativistic society there seem to be few propositions that can stand unchallenged. Certainly it would seem by all logic that such a proposition should be this one: *Accomplishment should be rewarded.* We are not going to refute that. But we feel it is important to take a close look at how the idea works out, in practice, in business, because the *means* that industry chooses to compensate for achievement, and penalize for failure, can often backfire. Too often pressure for achievement motivates people, not toward greater effort, but toward dishonesty.

When an employee is required to achieve a goal, quota, or budget, without having been given the means of accomplishing these ends, he is left with the alternatives of failing or resorting to dishonesty. We have seen too many instances of employees being forced to manipulate records to simulate achievement of unrealistic goals.

For years managers have felt increasingly burdened by the manifold tasks of controlling all of the functions under their jurisdiction. How does a manager, for example, handle a complex entity, and yet achieve the serenity of mind required to face decisions clearly, sift data judiciously, plan accurately from the long view? It is a tall order—and certainly the manager cannot do it if he must be continually looking over the shoulders of his subordinates. And this is why the concept of *management by objectives* is so welcome.

Management by objectives was conceived primarily as a means toward the better *development* of managerial talent. It is exemplified by Peter Drucker's injunction (in *The Practice of Management*) to "give full scope of individual strength and responsibility, and at the same time to give common direction to establish teamwork." It is not so much a new concept as a shifting of emphasis from means to ends, a reordering of priorities so that the management function begins with a clear definition of what is to be achieved. The mission starts with the description of the target.

In his book, *Management By Objectives,* David E. Olsson wrote:

> Management-by-objectives is an effective base from which to develop a practical management system. . . . Broad company objectives must be continually re-examined by the board and the management together. The results of these deliberations are the spring from which operating objectives flow. . . . Successful managers who carry out these activities are aware that objectives must be clear, concrete, free from vague terms, and attainable within a reasonable length of time.

But in translating this attractive concept into their own terms, working managers have tended more and more to talk, not of management by objectives, but management by *results*. If "results" is to be accepted as a synonym for "objectives," we are not discussing a point in semantics. We are changing the thrust of the concept.

The subordinate is assigned a job. He tries to do it.

Management examines the results, and if the results are not up to expectation, the subordinate is in trouble. This is not quite what the advocates of "management by objectives" have in mind. They see the approach more as a motivational factor. Results should be measured in terms of achievement. If results fall short of expectations, the standards should be realistically modified or the program abandoned. But, in practice, it does not always work out this way. The program may not be modified or discontinued, but the man in charge of it may be fired. So for top management, the concept seems to be a simplified way to gauge the value of middle-management talent on the payroll; but for the manager in the middle, the approach is a means of putting him on a very hot spot. He is being measured by results, so he has to deliver results, or at least he has to *appear* to deliver results. How he achieves them is left up to him.

A classic example of what can stem from the demand for results comes, not from business, but from the international area. Leo Cherne, executive director of the Research Institute of America and former director of the International Rescue Committee, has told of the occasion several years ago when American officials asked top officers in the then-ruling Vietnamese government how the pacification program was going in a certain area. The Vietnamese disclosed that 20 villages had been pacified. This was a thorough disappointment to the men from Washington, and the Vietnamese were told: "Absolutely unsatisfactory. When we come back in six months we want you to be able to tell us that 250 villages are under the pacification program."

Sure enough, in six months the Americans returned, and the Vietnamese told them that 250 villages had been pacified. The officials went back to Washington in jubilation and made their report, which was greeted as palpable evidence that the pacification program was working well. But soon disturbing news began to come in from the field; and the Vietnamese were queried once again: "You told us that there were 250 villages; we think the figure is still closer to 20." The Vietnamese shrugged. "Of course," they replied, "it is still close to 20. But we thought you wanted us to tell you that it was 250."

When top management wants to hear news of progress, and a man's job depends upon that news, he is likely to deliver what top management wants to hear. And he may not be too scrupulous about the way he does this.

We are conditioning our children to do this, too. In a report issued by the United States Junior Chamber of Commerce, the American school system came in for some critical observation. The report quotes a teacher: "There's too much emphasis on grades and tests, not enough on individual ability. Lots of kids cheat because they just can't do the work." Children attest to this. A fourteen-year-old girl: "Some parents say, 'If you fail, you can't go out for a month.' I know one boy whose father keeps threatening to take him out of school if he doesn't do better. All the kids are afraid of what their parents will say if they don't get good marks."

A sixteen-year-old girl admits that all the students in her class cheat regularly: "Kids get in a tight spot and cheat once. If they're not caught, they do it again and again. It's an atmosphere. No one cheated freshman year. After that it started, very little at first, but it spread tremendously. I was kind of shocked in the beginning. But everyone does it. First it's a glance at somebody's paper, then giving answers, then crib notes."

"It's an atmosphere." The atmosphere consists principally of increasing pressure for high performance, coupled with increasing latitude about the means by which results are to be achieved. A similar situation confronts the manager who is told, directly or by implication, that he had better deliver—or else.

There is a certain type of executive who, at a particular stage of his career and his life, is susceptible to this pressure, and who may turn to cheating as a means of delivering the results which he so desperately needs to hold his job. He is past forty. He has been with the company for what is beginning to seem like a long time. He earns a good salary, maybe $30,000 or more, but he has never gone as high as he hoped he would go. Certainly he has not advanced for some time.

"Middle-age megrims," is how Dr. Mortimer Feinberg, president of The Organizational Behavior Institute and widely known lecturer and writer on industrial psychology, describes this state of mind. When middle-age megrims set in, a man starts to look back, not forward; down, not up. He looks back in regret for lost opportunities: "If I had gone into partnership with Bob Walters ten years ago, I'd have it made by now. He's making a fortune. I could kick myself for not grabbing the chance when I had it." This man regards with increasing resentment the young "comers" who seem to be threatening his position: "They move these kids along too damn fast these days. They've got no respect for experience. They come out with these hair-brained schemes and management falls all over them." He looks down in fear: "Who'll hire me if I lose out here? Of course, they'd give me my severance, but things are tight; I don't know how I can keep going if I'm put on the bench."

He has never been a brilliant performer, but he works hard, never rocks the boat, and if the results he achieved were not spectacular, well, management could be tolerant about that. He is doing his best. And long and devoted service must count for something.

But now the picture has changed. The management may be under growing pressure from shareholders and may be increasingly impatient about lackluster performance. Or, there may be new management, possibly as the result of a merger or an acquisition. Or, the new and harsher light in which this man's efforts are regarded may simply be a function of the current emphasis upon maximum results, with decreasing attention paid to how they are obtained. In any event, the manager is now being judged by a new set of standards. And he begins to worry. He has not, for years, shared the working part of his existence with his wife, so now when he tries to talk over his problems, her apparent lack of understanding only annoys him more. His physical well-being is affected; he feels tired all the time. And his sexual potency drops off. Benjamin B. Wolman, a New York psychoanalyst whose practice consists heavily of executives and executives' wives, has seen, over and over again, the effect of job anxiety on husband-wife relationships: the man "comes home so tense that he shows little sexual interest. The normal affection goes out of the relationship. Sex becomes forced and scarce. The two are bed enemies, not mates."

All this has a devastating effect on the manager. He does not attribute his troubles to the natural inroads of middle age, nor to an inevitable change in the way business is done. He smolders with growing resentment, and blames all on the top management of his company. They have no appreciation for the years of loyal effort he has given them; they don't care what happens to a man; results are the only thing that matters to them. The company becomes the enemy. And enemies deserve whatever befalls them.

Now this man has yet another reason to rig his performance figures and cheat the organization. He is struggling to hang onto his job, which means a great deal more to him than a regular paycheck. It is his manhood; it is his life. That is one reason. But there is also the motive of revenge. The bosses have hurt him; he is in a position to retaliate. He is indeed in such a position, because management, while admonishing him that he must deliver satisfactory results, is at the same time giving him greater latitude. And this latitude, conceived as part of an effective new motivational approach, becomes a clear field for dishonesty.

Let's examine a typical case. Charles Brennan is divisional vice-president for production in a decentralized corporation. Brennan's background is mechanical engineering. He started with the company seventeen years prior as a sales engineer, but found after a couple of years in the field that selling was not for him. Details and processes came easily to him; but not dealing with customers. The easy give and take in buyers' offices, the camaraderie of the luncheon table, the infighting over deliveries, percentages, and (sometimes) kickbacks made him uncomfortable.

So he requested a transfer into plant engineering. Here he was in his element. He evolved no brilliant new methods; but the dogged way in which he would chip away at a problem until he had a solution impressed his superiors. However, Brennan did not permit himself to become a specialist in a narrow field. He set out to learn all that he could about every phase of production, even to the extent of taking night courses to acquire the necessary feel for bookkeeping and record-keeping.

Brennan is a solid citizen—a man the company can depend upon. Other men, perhaps smarter and more imaginative, came and went. Brennan plugged along steadily until he reached his present eminence—a high-salaried, responsible job. Brennan and his wife and family enjoy a beautiful home, pleasant vacations, and most of the good things of life.

Although it was never explicitly discussed, a tacit assumption has grown in the company's top management that Brennan is not going to be promoted beyond his present job. Brennan himself has worried about this, but he has never permitted it to upset him. For about a year he had been reporting to a new executive vice-president, Ray Peal. Peal is a devotee of the "new management"—a scientific administrator who thinks of himself as understanding people and knowing what it takes to motivate them but who sets high standards and does whatever is necessary to get the job done.

After some study Peal concluded that Brennan's operation could be more productive than it had been. He called Brennan in and launched into what was—to Peal—a long, productive discussion. Goals were talked over and decisions made. These goals were not arbitrarily established by Peal; Brennan was given every chance to participate in the goal-setting process. So when Brennan finally agreed to some higher production quotas, Peal quite sincerely assumed that the other man was speaking objectively on the basis of free choice and unclouded judgment.

The trouble with this assumption is that it is much easier for the boss to view such a conversation as a chat between equals than it is for the subordinate. In talking about goals, Brennan felt an unaccustomed tension. There were a lot of reasons, he felt, why certain goals were not altogether realistic. He voiced some of his reservations, but Peal responded with persuasive arguments and a smiling assurance that of course Brennan was capable of delivering what was wanted. Brennan came out of the goal-setting meeting with the vague feeling that he had put himself on the spot.

And he had. Production did not go up to the extent

that had been anticipated. Brennan talked to Peal about it once or twice, but Peal's response boiled down to: "You know how I feel about it, Charley. I'm not going to stick my nose into an area that you handle so superbly. You've got the ball and I'm sure you can run with it. Any backing you need, you've got it from me. Otherwise, Charley, it's your ball game."

Brennan began to think about that: "It's your ball game." It *was* his ball game. Nobody knew all the ins and outs of production, and of the reporting of production, as well as he did. Sitting in his office, idly playing with some unsatisfactory figures, it passed through his mind that it would be very easy to make them look like *satisfactory* figures. Brennan let the thought slip out of his mind. But it kept coming back. One afternoon, telling himself that he was just "noodling," Charles Brennan sat down and began to "play" with the inventory sheets. It started, or so he told himself, as a kind of game just to see what could be done. But it soon developed into more than that.

Brennan began to spend less time with his supervisors, more time in his office playing with figures. And he soon became a skillful, sophisticated manipulator— not for money, but to hang onto his job. Nothing went into Brennan's pocket. His energy and expertise were devoted to kidding management into thinking that his department was turning out more than it was. Brennan, formerly a loyal and dedicated man, was impelled to this course of action because his fear and his frustration made him desperate and angry.

Top management is now happy looking at figures that are pleasing. It has delegated the job to Brennan and, so far as it knows, Brennan is doing the job. Nobody checks. And Brennan is breezing along. By now he has it all down to a science. He can write up his week's production figures by lunch time on Thursday—and make sure that they are high enough to pass muster. If there is any problem he can add to the stockpile by dipping into reserves, rejects, customer returns.

So, with its hands-off, look-only-at-the-results policy, management is letting Brennan commit fraud on a major and destructive scale. Of course, it occasionally crosses their collective mind that dishonesty is possible. But the thought is generalized, never particularized to an individual—certainly not to such a trusted, long-time functionary as Charley Brennan. And, if something is going wrong, the accountants will catch it. This near-superstitious faith in the accounting profession can result in the company paying taxes on non-existent profits.

Management too often harbors the mistaken impression that standard auditing procedures are adequate to expose theft. Although accountants sometimes do uncover dishonesty, they are not in the business of ferreting out fraud and theft, per se. Their obligation is merely to establish the validity of a firm's financial statement. *Fortune* remarks that "some members of the profession talk ambitiously of the 'principles' on which accounting practices rest, and of the 'postulates' on which the principles rest—as though the whole edifice had been constructed logically, like a theorem in geometry. Yet, there is no definitive list of principles or postulates, and many of the practices have simply evolved *ad hoc.*"

Very often, opportunists find it easy to bypass *conventional* accounting controls. In fact, over-reliance upon traditional devices for controlling inventory of materials, tools, and work-in-progress can contribute to a firm's vulnerability. This explains why *unconventional* auditing techniques, specifically geared to uncover theft and manipulation, are needed to supplement conventional procedures.

In management's wishful thinking about the efficacy

of accountancy against major fraud, they have the conviction that a manager can falsely report his production for only a limited period of time before the fateful moment of reckoning: Inventory Day.

How does Charles Brennan handle inventory day? At the basis of Brennan's approach lies the fact that the inventory-taker understands figures, but is not overly-knowledgeable about the technical terms bandied about in the business. So the inventory-taker arrives, and Brennan takes him through the warehouse personally. Brennan shows him an item in stock: "That's a gold-bonded switch," he says, "Number 108." The inventory-taker makes some notes, counts the items in stock. There are 5,000 of them.

The book figure for the Number 108 gold-bonded switch is $20. So, simple arithmetic credits Brennan's department with a $100,000 inventory in this item. But, in actuality, the 108 switch looks to the untutored eye just like the 708 brass-bonded switches, which have a value of $8. And it is the 708 that Brennan has shown the man with the clipboard. The inventory has been falsified by $60,000.

Management sets up the motivation for this kind of deception when it concentrates almost exclusively upon results. It provides the opportunity by maintaining a laissez-faire policy toward how those results are achieved. But it takes something else, a catalyst, to set the machinery for theft in motion.

That catalyst is a *communications block* between middle management and top management.

Charles Brennan tried to talk about his problems to Ray Peal. But Peal did not respond; of course, from Peal's point of view there was no communications problem. He and Brennan had talked over the objectives, and Brennan had given every indication that he understood them. For too many members of top management, here is where communications end. It is a potentially costly mistake to think this way.

Communications should not be thought of as a transmission belt that always carries a full load of meaningful exchange. *Good* communications is rather a state of corporate mind, a willingness and eagerness that superior and subordinate *relate* to each other, even if they do not have favorable news to impart.

It is futile to try to prevent manipulated results by setting up elaborate controls. Such controls may stultify initiative. But when a manager is told that he will be judged by results, this should not mean that he is cut off from every opportunity to talk over his methods and his problems. Nor should it imply that he will be penalized for admitting that he has a problem. The man who comes in and talks to this superior about his problems may cause some annoyance, but if he does not talk them out he may resolve his conflicts in a way that costs the company hundreds of thousands of dollars.

8 REVERSE INCENTIVES IN MERCHANDISING

INCENTIVES FOR PERFORMANCE CAN BE INCENTIVES FOR CRIME

Every employee needs motivation to perform better. But certain kinds of motivation spur employees in a different direction. They provide both the motivation and the opportunity to steal. Some of the risks in popular incentive programs far exceed the value of any possible gains.

We find many examples of material incentives in the retail industry. For example, some publishers attempt to influence sales clerks in bookstores to recommend their books to undecided shoppers. What could be a more logical way of winning the goodwill of sales clerks than to give them the publishers' own books as gifts? So the young man or woman who works in a bookstore may receive quite a few volumes free, whether they are ever likely to be read or not.

More than one large chain of bookstores maintains the gracious policy of permitting employees who receive as gifts books that they have already read to exchange those books for others from the store's shelves. Of course, the formulators of this policy had in mind Christmas and birthday gifts, not the incentive books sent out by publishers to the clerks' homes. Clerks sell the incentive books, or exchange them for other books that are more saleable. Either way, the publishers' practice lets the clerks go into the book business for themselves.

Here is one way in which an attempt to promote business results in self-competition and a diminution of business, to an impressive degree.

The use of "spiffs"—sometimes called "push money" or "PM's"—is a deeply imbedded practice in many industries producing consumer products. For example, spiffs are common in the mattress business. The manufacturer will pay say $5 to the manager of the bedding department for every one of the maker's mattresses sold. So, an aggressive department manager who is in need of some quick ready cash secures store approval for a blitzkrieg campaign in mattresses. For a week he floods the trading area with newspaper ads and radio spots, offering large markdowns—mail and phone orders accepted.

The results are extremely gratifying. Indeed, the manager finds that he is 140 mattresses short of actual sales. From previous experience in overselling, the manager knows that this kind of response is ephemeral; customers will not wait. Instead, they will cancel the order. But if this happens, the manager will be out $700 in spiffs.

The answer is simple. He fills each order by shipping out any mattress he has in stock—wrong sizes, wrong types. By the time the customers get around to returning them—a mattress being not quite as easy to return as a pair of cuff links—he will have the correct mattress in stock. And that is the way it works out. The complaints begin to come in, and eventually the unsuitable merchandise trickles back. A lot of the returned mattresses are not in saleable condition any more. A dress that has been tried on can be sold again; not so a mattress that has been slept on. And in desperation some customers have slept on them or torn or soiled them before finding out that they received the wrong mattress.

Finally, the customers all get the mattresses they ordered. And of course the manager has long since spent his push money. The loser is the store—in ruined merchandise, extra handling costs, and impaired customer goodwill.

Spiffs can take the form of money or merchandise. A national TV manufacturer decides to run a promotion on a certain line of color TV sets: "Mr. Manager, sell twelve sets and you get the thirteenth from us— FREE." So one manager, we will not call him typical but we will not say that he is absolutely unique, goes to work on the telephone. Is he calling new prospects who do not own a color TV and who might be considered in the market? No. Too much wasted time and spinning of wheels in a procedure like that (although doubtlessly this is the approach envisioned by those who thought up the promotion).

As he sits at the telephone, the manager has before him a list of customers who *have* bought color TV sets, *any* brand, within the past three weeks. To the casual observer this might seem the least likely way to generate new business. But not the way this manager handles it: "You bought an RCA," he says to a customer. "I'm calling to find out if you are *completely* happy with it. Have you noticed anything—any problems at all?" When the query is put this way, quite a few customers will say something like, "Well, the reception is not quite what I had hoped it would be." This is the manager's opening: "That's why I'm calling you. We want our customers to be completely happy." He may add a few more words to imply vaguely that others have complained. Then: "Now, we've got a special on another national brand. It's a truly fine set, all solid state, best engineered unit on the market; and I'm able to offer you today a very good deal on it—$39 less than your present set and one year's free service. I can have it installed and a $39 refund in your hands this afternoon."

Within three days the manager has sold twelve sets. Of course, the store has taken back twelve other sets, with all the expense and damage that this entails. But the manager has won his prize, the thirteenth set. Naturally, he already owns a color TV: of all people, he would have one. So he then sells the thirteenth set to a store customer and pockets the money.

Sometimes a salesperson does not even have to do any selling to earn a spiff. For example, it is commonplace in the perfume and cosmetic business to offer push money, but the payment of the spiff is based on the amount of reorders. A saleswoman gets her payment, not for how much she sells across the counter, but rather for how much stock is shipped into the store. So a case of skin cream or cologne comes into the department. It gets "lost"—months later it is found in the housewares stockroom. Another order must be placed immediately; it may well be a "rush," shipped in by air express. There is no way that the store can claim that the earlier merchandise was not delivered; receiving records show that it was. So the store steadily orders more products than it is selling; and the saleswoman is getting her spiffs without even bothering to push the merchandise.

Sales managers are always looking for new ways to motivate salesmen to superior effort through the application of incentives. The prizes have gotten bigger and bigger. And the contests do seem to have an effect; more business is written during the contest period than at other times. Yet, when the end of the year rolls around, net results are not quite up to management's expectations based on the monthly sales figures.

Here is an example of why this happens. Harry

Howell is a detail man for a pharmaceutical company. He is going down the homestretch in a contest. On the line is a trip to Europe for Howell and his wife. Mrs. Howell is already selecting her wardrobe; but Harry is worried. He needs to sell another $35,000 worth of business, but he is running out of leads and time.

So, dapper as always, Harry Howell breezes into the office of the purchasing agent at one of the larger hospitals in his territory: "Honey," he says to Mrs. Irvin, the purchasing agent, "you've just got to give me another order. Fifteen thousand would be fine, but twenty thousand would be even better." She replies, "Sweetheart, you're losing your memory. You were here two weeks ago and I gave you all kinds of orders. I'm overstocked now."

But Harry Howell has an answer. "Don't worry about it. With your order and a couple of others, I'll win that trip to Europe for sure. You tell me what you want me to bring back for you and I'll get it—something real nice. And when I come back, I'll show you how to charge back the merchandise by claiming it arrived contaminated, or some other reason why you can't accept it and we take the shipment back. No strain; you'll be doing me a big favor and I'll do one for you."

Howell has been very nice to Mrs. Irvin in the past; she feels that reciprocation is in order, particularly since there will be something in it for her. So, she agrees. Not surprisingly, many of the other detail men battling to win the contest are doing the same thing. Volume is very big this month; returns and credits will be enormous two months later.

There is another point that must be made about incentives, bonuses, and motivators. Very soon people begin to take them for granted. This means that, as with many other artificial stimulants, successively larger doses are required to achieve the same effect. But if for any reason the level of incentives is cut back, the withdrawal symptoms can be painful for the worker and calamitous for his employer.

This effect is noted time and again, especially in a period of slowdown or recession. The economic crunch hits the executive, whose incentives are suddenly eliminated—his bonus, his profit-sharing plan, or his stock options, which have become valueless. Employees who have come to expect the periodic bonuses, and count on them—not as extras, but as necessary income to put their children through college or to pay off mortgages on homes—discover that they are in a serious bind.

The result in many cases is an upsurge in business crime. To mention just one of numerous tragic instances, a purchasing agent was approaching retirement and he was looking forward to his golden years of leisure. He had it all planned: Florida sun, fishing, trips to places he had never seen. Then he learned that his own retirement nest egg had declined 39 percent. Very little of what he had hoped for was possible now. He had always been honest, scrupulously conscious of his position of trust and of the moral imperatives governing civilized behavior. In a flood of disappointment and despair, all of this was forgotten.

The purchasing agent had a little time on the job remaining to him. He used it to enter into arrangements with shady suppliers, to "arrange" bids, and to indulge in all of the practices from which he had refrained throughout an honorable career. In a few months the company was out $50,000. The purchasing agent was caught, however, and he now has very little to look forward to for the rest of his life.

There is another form of incentive employed by corporations with independent contractors. It is familiarly known as "cost-plus," an arrangement under which the contractor is guaranteed his costs plus an agreed-on profit.

Here is how cost-plus operated in the case of a gigantic U.S.-based steel fabricator involved in the pipeline expansion northward to Canada and Alaska. The company determined to build a large installation in British Columbia. The contract was awarded on a sealed-bid, hard-money basis. Under "hard money" the contractor agrees to do the job for a fixed sum. If his costs run higher than his projections, that is his tough luck. He is obligated to complete the job to specifications for the agreed-upon price.

The fabrication giant let the contract for about $8 million—quite a low bid, they thought, but the contractor was reputable and gave every indication of being able to complete the job as agreed. However, as the work progressed, the company found that another addition was needed. Obviously, this was not covered in the original contract, and time was too short to obtain bids. Besides, the contractor was already on the job with his machinery and skilled craftsmen. Since it was a little difficult to determine exactly how much the addition would cost, the contractor's estimate of approximately $1 million was accepted, and the addition was awarded on a cost-plus basis. The additional work was small in comparison to the main job, but it offered a large loophole to the contractor. Perhaps the contractor anticipated that something like this would happen when he submitted his original low bid. Indeed, maybe he had contacts in the steel-fabricating company who led him to anticipate this development.

The contractor brought in 50 additional men, with equipment and supplies. They signed in under the cost-plus arrangement. All the invoices were credited to the cost-plus deal. But, a half hour after signing in, most of these men were switched over to the hard-money job. Now, the contractor was getting a free ride on the main job, and handling the cost-plus job on a hand-to-mouth basis. He wound up making a very comfortable profit under his tight hard-money bargain. The cost-plus work ran far beyond the original estimate —to $1.5 million—but the contractor had no worries on that score.

Oddly enough, the introduction of premium promotions can also uncover long-standing underhanded operations that can destroy the image the firm has painstakingly built.

Witness an oil company that offered its retailers high-ticket appliances if they increased sales of the company's top line of gas. Sales results were enormous. However, the merchandise awarded in a number of locations was far above the amount of premium gas that was being pumped. Careful study revealed that delivery men were in collusion with retailers— pumping low-octane gas into storage tanks for premium gas and splitting the profits.

When a blue chip company decided to enter the credit card business, it offered each new customer that signed up a silver dollar key chain as a bonus. The premium obtained the desired results. Then a steady flow of complaints began coming in. Over 1,000 disillusioned people claimed that the company reneged on the premium offer. The ensuing investigation revealed that two mail room clerks were capturing the $3.50 premium product before it was mailed.

The fault here lies not only with two bad apples in the barrel but with management. The company adopted an intelligently designed premium promotion and utilized it effectively. Then by ignoring the fact that premium merchandise, by its very nature, is highly desirable and costly, the company had allowed it to be handled through the normal channel of distribution.

Companies that set up programs for the distribution of premium merchandise in sales promotion contests are particularly vulnerable. The carefully nurtured image that established premiums as a vital ingredient in today's marketing programs—that of receiving something "free" for buying a favorite shampoo or of winning a "free" television for selling over sales quota —is the very element that is bilking corporations of millions of dollars. The knowledge that hi-fi's, golf clubs, cameras, and a variety of other highly desirable merchandise is being given away has become an overpowering temptation to normally honest company employees to get in on the giveaways. Their rationale is: "It's free. No one will be losing anything if I take an item or two."

A candy company that had never lost a case of bubble gum was shocked to discover that $70,000 worth of premium products were missing from its warehouse. The company executives failed to realize that the premium merchandise had a far greater value than their own products and should never have been stored and shipped with the same logistical format.

9 KICKBACKS: A $5-BILLION RIPOFF

How widespread is the payoff in business? Executives in industry increasingly are wondering whether it is possible to conduct their business these days without paying off someone—government or labor officials, purchasing agents, store managers, or others who are in a position to influence dollars-and-cents decisions.

It's difficult for legitimate businessmen to stay in business today because of the pervasive growth of kickbacks. They're damned if they do and damned if they don't.

Never have kickbacks, bribes, and conflicts of interest been such dominant factors in the conduct of business. Pressures resulting from competition generally drive prices to marginal levels. In almost all fields there is not enough margin between cost and selling price to support surreptitious payments designed to generate business. When gratuities are the accepted practice, the buyer invariably compromises either by accepting a lower quality product or a short count, or by paying more than the same goods would cost elsewhere. He can no longer complain about late deliveries, refusals to accept returns for whatever the reason, or the absence of discounts on quantity purchases or for prompt payment.

The significance of this is clear. Gratuities, or to put

it more bluntly, kickbacks, are an added cost to the purchaser, rather than an additional expense to the vendor of the merchandise.

Although this truth should be self-evident, there are still a surprisingly large number of executives, owners, and managers who prefer to close their eyes to the fact that the people who handle their procurement— whether it be the purchasing agent, chief of maintenance, traffic manager, or others—may be the recipient of "gifts."

A vendor should be able to hold its accounts through the quality of its wares and through the honest values and good service it offers. Legitimate suppliers should not be forced to compete with those who engage in under-the-table deals and who can hold an account only by offering unethical and illegal inducements.

In many instances, executives have been known to rationalize that, if this fringe benefit were eliminated, a higher wage would have to be paid their employees. "Take care of my buyer" is an all too common expression. This kind of thinking is both dangerous and fallacious.

Furthermore, many entrepreneurs who own their companies encourage under-the-table deals as a tax avoidance device.

The spiraling costs of kickbacks and conflicts of interest are passed on through the economy by manufacturer, wholesaler, and retailer to the consumer.

The very practices set up by management to promote business—such as variable commission, cash sales, contests, samples, liberal return privileges, credits, and advertising "allowances"—are exploited by their own marketing personnel to siphon off cash for kickbacks. In this way, marketing men meet their quotas and earn big bonuses at the expense of their employers.

The forms in which kickbacks are given have become

increasingly sophisticated—loans, consulting fees, false invoicing, stockbroker accounts, yearly auto rentals, use of credit cards, paid vacations, golf tournaments with lavish prizes, country club dues, gift certificates, charge accounts, and even works of art. Engineers, purchasing agents, and buyers have become knowledgeable about circumventing established safeguards and discouraging reputable businessmen in order to protect favored vendors and friends.

Suppose a small manufacturer has developed a new product which he feels has a great potential. He contacts a buyer of a major chain store to evaluate the product, get guidance as to market acceptability, and if all goes well, to offer it to the chain on an exclusive basis. The buyer leaves him very enthusiastic, very hopeful. "It's a good idea; it's a good product." However, there are too many frills; costs must be reduced, and the manufacturer must come up with a simplified design. He is told to return within a week with a modified design, production cost data, and other details. The manufacturer is so enthusiastic that he neglects his regular business to have the required information on time.

When he returns the following Monday the buyer casually looks it over and says, "Leave it; I'm very busy with meetings today and I will get back to you just as soon as I get a chance to evaluate it." The buyer promptly calls the manufacturer's competitor with whom he has been doing business and whom he has known socially for the past fifteen years. Ultimately the small manufacturer's brainchild is rejected and, to make matters worse, his competitor comes out with a similar product.

The big boom in kickbacks began in World War II when prosperity and a shortage of merchandise encouraged businessmen to grab the goods and make any deals they could. The spread of mass marketing techniques, with heavy emphasis on name brands and nationwide television, has increased opportunities for kickbacks. Salesmen of goods in heavy demand, for example, are in a position to ask for or be offered favors.

Competition for shelf space in supermarkets also gives rise to kickbacks. Authorities say bribes have reached the point where nationally advertised soft drinks, beers, and other well-known products are kept off shelves unless vendors of these products buy display, shelf space, and location by paying off the store manager, grocery manager, or even district manager on some predetermined basis, such as a stated amount per case, gifts from catalogues, or free goods for their personal use. Manufacturers of these brands, when apprised of such matters, comment that they have no control over the distributors and dealers who handle their products.

Often the blandishments of bribers are too tempting to resist, as a young purchasing agent for a technical-goods firm learned. Invited, along with his wife, by a supplier to a new-products exhibition in Las Vegas, he found a luxury suite awaiting him, plus expensive gifts. When he lost $3,000 the first night at the gambling tables, the supplier paid for the losses.

Two airline executives were charged with taking thousands in "10 percent kickbacks" from companies they hired to do promotional work for the airline. One of the men pleaded guilty; the other disappeared.

An engineering consultant was indicted in New Orleans for allegedly offering $60,000 to get a bridge design job. An architect there says, "The system down here is that 10 percent is considered the normal 'finder's fee' for public work."

A group of American companies has been indicted

on charges of paying kickbacks to the U.S. purchasing agent for an Italian manufacturer. The federal prosecutor claimed that a number of executives paid the buyer $200,000 to arrange purchase of metals and aircraft parts from their firms.

And in the most spectacular example in our history, the Vice President of the United States resigned just before pleading no contest to income tax evasion that was an outgrowth of a kickback scheme.

Why do so many employees take kickbacks? Authorities cite various reasons—greed, revenge, the feeling that it is necessary to meet competition or get ahead in a company. Many caught taking kickbacks say, "Everybody's doing it."

The confessions that show up in our reports of kickback schemes offer such reasons for accepting them as:

• "I saved the company $100,000 on that purchase. Don't I deserve a slice?"
• "You've got to play along if you want a piece of the action."
• "I'm entitled to the benefits I get under the table. It's not costing my company anything."
• "I'm not in a profit-sharing plan like my boss, and I do all the work."
• "It's no different from tipping a waiter or the maître d' for good service."

The following case histories are illustrative of kickback transactions we uncovered:

A Fixed Percentage Payoff
While engaged in a study of a mass catering organization, our engineers heard persistent rumors that the purchasing agent would deal only with wholesalers who paid him off. Upon being apprised of this, the top

executive did not deny the possibility, but shrugged off the insinuation with the remark, "It couldn't amount to much, and besides, it doesn't matter to me how those suppliers choose to spend their money."

This executive changed his tune when, as the result of further investigation, the purchasing agent was confronted with our findings and a full confession of his multifarious activities was obtained. The buyer admitted that inferior merchandise was accepted while he authorized payment for premium grades. In return, the vendors paid him a fixed percentage of their monthly billing, ranging from 3 percent from grocery wholesalers to 7 percent from produce wholesalers.

The Early Retirement

At an institution of higher learning, the head of maintenance applied for retirement four years before he reached the mandatory retirement age. The suspicious school officials called for an investigation which revealed that over a period of more than twenty years this man had received a rake-off from almost every plumbing and electrical supply house, hardware store, lumberyard, and outside contractor with whom he did business. He had accumulated such a large nest egg that he could afford to retire early on a reduced pension and live out his last years in luxury.

Truckling to the Trucker

A textile-processing company was victimized by their traffic manager, who received $500 a month from the trucking company that handled the bulk of their deliveries. In order to "earn" the fee, this manager approved and passed for payment padded invoices, duplicate invoices, erroneous freight and demurrage charges, and other excessive items.

The Case of the Hungry Chef

During an operational survey at a prominent hotel, our methods analysts discovered that the executive chef held "open house" every Tuesday afternoon. Representatives from the various food purveyors came at that time to pay him off. The purchasing agent had learned long before that all his orders must be placed with certain favored vendors. Otherwise the chef would refuse the delivery, claiming that the merchandise was inferior; to add insult to injury, he deliberately kept meats and vegetables out of the refrigerator so that by the time the non-favored vendor's truck came to pick up the rejected items, they were already spoiled. When the vendor complained, the chef's remark was, "If I kept it in the refrigerator, it would stink up the place."

Culture for Sale

I recently visited a soft-goods manufacturer and noticed a number of reproductions of fine oil paintings on the walls of his office. I said to him, "I didn't know you were a lover of the arts." He replied: "I'm not. This wall is Picasso; this wall is Andrew Wyeth, and that wall is Monet. My big chain store buyers get a picture from the 'Picasso' wall. Smaller accounts get a selection from the 'Wyeth' or 'Monet' walls."

Second Best, but He Tries Harder

A sales manager in a printing firm revealed how he pays off to get business from brokerage houses, banks, and insurance companies. He said: "The people I deal with are underpaid, high livers, and good drinkers. I discovered an easy method of kicking back. I give them all automobiles—a 26-month rental from an auto rental service. Of course, it's never rented under their names. I make the payments every month—and the month I don't get their business, I stop the payments. They've become accustomed to the car. They haven't got $5,000 to go out and buy one."

The Defense: "Am I My Salesmen's Keeper?"

Confronted with the accusation that gratuities were paid to the purchasing agents of various airlines, hospitals, hotels, and other institutions with whom his company was doing business, one wholesaler attempted to defend himself by claiming that such gratuities were the work of his salesmen, and "What they do with their commissions is none of my concern."

This attempt to shirk responsibility is an example of the fallacious thinking which is widely prevalent. When salesmen attempt to "buy" business, it most certainly is, or should be, the concern of the company that employs them. Above all, as we have sought to demonstrate, it should be of vital importance to the company that purchased the goods.

Tax Subterfuge

Vendors who distribute kickbacks on a large scale are faced with the problem of how to show these expenditures on their books in order to claim them as deductions on their income tax reports. As these pay-offs are generally made in cash with no supporting documentation, the items are not an acceptable deduction from income when subjected to scrutiny by auditors. Consequently, in recent years there has been a tendency to place the purchasing agent, food buyer, or other recipient on the vendor's payroll. This trend has accelerated as a result of the more severe accounting procedures required under tax laws.

We recently heard of a vendor who took a buyer to lunch and said: "I'll continue paying you five thousand dollars a year for business, but I'll have to carry you on my books as an independent salesman and show the payment as a commission. You should include this sum in your income tax report. Let me know what this costs you, depending upon your tax bracket, and I'll make up this additional amount in cash."

When vendors resort to a subterfuge such as this, however, they become more vulnerable to exposure as these surreptitious transactions can be more easily traced and a determination made of the actual sums involved. The rationalization here, of course, is that the payment is really an earned commission.

In another instance, a chain store buyer told a dress manufacturer that he needed a $7,000 loan in order to pay for his children's college tuition. The manufacturer pointed out that he had not even begun to cut the goods, much less ship them, and that he would not be billing them for another six months. The buyer then intimated that he might cancel the order. The manufacturer could hardly let this happen, because, aside from the amounts involved, this was a pace-setter account which greatly influenced his decisions on the kind of fabric, texture and colors, he would purchase for the season. The manufacturer had to give himself a $10,000 raise in order to generate the funds to cover the so-called loan and the taxes thereon.

That some managers consider kickbacks to employees inimical to their company's interest is attested to by several recent civil suits initiated by department stores against both ex-employees and vendors. The actions maintain that illegal commissions, discounts, bribes, or kickbacks were made to induce buyers to make purchases of specific goods. The legal documents also charge that the manufacturers' selling prices were "loaded" to cover the bribe payments.

In two state court cases an aluminum products company won judgments totaling $1,297,390, including $162,500 in punitive damages, against former officers and their families for kickbacks received from suppliers over a ten-year period. Stating that their conduct was akin to embezzlement, the court awarded the plaintiff full restitution of sums received by the defendants, interest at 6 percent on the money from the time it was received, and punitive damages. In commenting on the conduct of the defendants, the court said: "All of them occupied positions of high trust and responsibility and were commensurately compensated for their work. Their willful and brazen conduct was plainly wrong and immoral."

Unfortunately, too many honest executives display a defeatist attitude with regard to the need to purge their companies of cheats, chiselers, and connivers. And it is precisely this attitude that has permitted the spread of deceptive practices. The desperate competitor often hides behind the industry's Code of Ethics which hangs prominently in his office, urging that all adhere to it while he bends every rule in the book. Unfortunately, other firms, which have the best of intentions, may be tempted to adopt similar methods with the result that the Code becomes meaningless.

The unflattering publicity that results from revelations of unethical conduct has adversely affected the public's once high regard for business leaders; our entire system of private enterprise is being subjected to the strong and merciless light of public opinion.

Hospitals and other semi-charitable or charitable institutions that wish to make a determined effort to eliminate kickbacks should not overlook the possibility that they themselves may be guilty of demanding excessive contributions from time to time from the vendors that service them. Regardless of how worthy the cause, there is a risk that the supplier may seek to retrieve this "forced" money by inflating prices or lowering quality, with the net result that the institution has really made a donation to itself.

On the other hand, we know of several nonprofit organizations that advised their vendors that gifts to employees would henceforth be prohibited and suggested that, instead, the vendor might wish to donate that sum to the institution. When an expense analysis survey was instituted in one hospital to determine its supply costs compared to those of other institutions, discrepancies that were revealed were sufficient to call for an investigation. Our audit findings proved that the purchasing agent rarely bothered to obtain competitive bids when making purchases. Price quotations were accepted on good faith, usually with the vendor at the reins. Orders were placed primarily on the basis of favors returned.

After the malpractices were brought to light, the hospital administrator deliberated on the course of corrective action to take. Rather than penalize the guilty vendors, he decided to distribute written notices announcing his awareness of past practices. He invited suppliers to send future donations to the hospital. The response was gratifying. One printer presented a check for $1,000. "This is not necessary to retain our business," the printer was told. "I appreciate that," he replied, "but it is something I want to do. I'm still ahead of the game. Kickbacks used to cost me $4,000 a year."

After the new purchasing procedures were installed, including the periodic review of bids by administrative personnel, the reduction in supply costs ultimately amounted to more than 32 percent.

Regardless of size and manner of presentation, business gifts invariably raise questions of business ethics.

Regardless of how insignificant the offering, there is always the danger that the practice will get out of hand. The only safe and proper course is the elimination of gift giving and receiving between employees and customers or suppliers. This practice is gaining wide acceptance, although many companies do permit their employees to accept presents providing the offering can be consumed in one day. To illustrate, under this rule a bottle of liquor would be considered acceptable, but not a case.

Increasingly large numbers of firms now send letters to their suppliers each November, pointing out that their employees are prohibited from accepting any gifts whatsoever and requesting the vendor's cooperation on this matter. Unfortunately, some companies that engage in this practice seem to feel that merely going through the motions of sending such a letter automatically relieves them of all further responsibility. Buyers on their staff look upon such notices with indifference. A typical reaction is: "This is fine. It will remind the vendors not to forget about me, and to send the gifts directly to my home."

The following are typical of such notices:

> Dear Supplier:
> We recognize that our past successes, as well as our future prosperity, are directly related to our good business relationships with companies such as yours. We believe that such meaningful associations are built on mutual respect and understanding.
> We have a policy that prohibits our employees from accepting gifts in any form from the companies with whom we do business. We need your help to implement the policy. Therefore, I ask that you please communicate this information to appropriate personnel in your organization.

As the year-end Holiday Season approaches, I want to thank you for helping us to make this a successful year. On behalf of all of our personnel, I send you and your associates best wishes for a joyous Christmas season and a bright New Year.

> Sincerely,
> Kingsley J. Jones, President
> International Industries, Ltd.

TO: ALL GUARDS
SUBJECT: EMPLOYEE GIFTS

In the past it has been a practice of outside vendors and suppliers to bring Christmas gifts for _____ employees and leave such gifts at the gate until picked up by the respective employees.

This letter is to advise you that we received instructions from the home office that this practice is no longer in effect. Therefore, I suggest that you use the following procedure:

Anyone desiring to leave a gift for an employee will be advised that plant procedure has been enacted so that these gifts cannot be left at the Gate House for distribution. You are to tactfully advise these people that the gifts are to be delivered to the employee's home and you are authorized to supply such address if needed.

This policy has no exceptions, regardless of rank or position.

If you have any questions or run into any problem connected with these instructions, you are requested to contact the writer.

This policy will go into effect upon receipt of this letter.

> DONALD L. DONALD
> General Manager

cc: All Dept. Heads
and Purchasing Agents

Some companies that do not forbid the acceptance of gratuities by employees nevertheless require that their people submit a list of all gifts they receive. These periodic reports, which state both the cash amounts and a valuation of any merchandise obtained, also indicate where the transaction took place. Although an employee can falsify such a report, this full-disclosure rule is bound to make him think twice before entering into an arrangement that is likely to be frowned upon by management. The report would have added impact value if submitted in the form of a sworn affidavit.

An even more extreme measure is to require vendors to sign an agreement to the effect that no gratuities of any kind, either in cash or merchandise, or favors, such as a personal loan, will be made to any of their employees. Vendors could also be required to stipulate that in the event any provision of this agreement is violated, they are liable for triple damages or other penalties. A bold and forthright step such as this is likely to produce the desired results.

Companies can also adopt other means of defense against kickbacks. As part of an employment agreement, they can require purchasing agents to provide them with financial statements or to authorize an investigation of the employee's financial assets. Full disclosure of financial resources is required by banks when they extend credit of several thousand dollars on a personal loan, or even on an installment loan amounting to only a few hundred dollars. There should be no timidity about requiring full disclosure from an employee who is to be given authority to spend anywhere from several thousand to several million dollars for his firm each year.

Such an understanding at the time of employment or promotion will underscore management's intention of enforcing a no-kickback policy rather than merely paying lip service to it. Although this tool may never be used, it is of considerable value as a psychological deterrent.

In addition to presenting a clear and firm statement of company policy, the employment agreement should spell out all the ramifications of a violation of the contract, including such matters as forfeiture of profit-sharing, effect upon retirement fund, and other benefits the company has paid for. The objective is to avoid litigation at a later date.

Unfortunately, there are very few laws concerning kickbacks, except for those that bar bribes to government or union officials. Only a handful of states have laws involving commercial bribery, and in most of those states it's classified as a misdemeanor or an offense, where the penalty is no more than would apply for spitting on the floor.

Of course, those who take and give kickbacks are subject to civil suit. But this has not served as much of a deterrent because of management's frequent inability to thoroughly document its case and its reluctance to press the matter in the absence of legislation.

We need uniform legislation around the country, perhaps by federal statute. We must pass laws that would declare that it is a criminal act to offer or take kickbacks.

But I still feel that any laws enacted will not be enough. We need tougher action by business itself. Key executives of an organization have to assume responsibility for how its agents, representatives, and marketing people do business. A top executive can't say, "If my salesman makes payoffs out of his own pocket, it's no concern of mine." He can't say, "I need the business badly," and close his eyes to kickbacks and payoffs. If the top people in a company don't set and enforce standards of honesty, there's little hope that anyone else will within the organization.

The top executive must issue clear and specific guide-lines, listing all the different forms of kickbacks and bribes and barring them. He must say, "We will go after anybody who's involved in kickbacks or conflicts of interest, even if it's going to cost us some business."

Following are policy statements on conflicts of interest, ethical business conduct, and purchasing policy that have been adopted by some organizations. We do not recommend any particular statement, but offer them here as possible models:

CONFLICTS OF INTEREST—ETHICAL BUSINESS CONDUCT

Example A

In general, a conflict of interest may be defined as an activity or interest which is inconsistent with or opposed to the legitimate best interests of the Company. The Company naturally expects from its employees complete and undivided loyalty to its interests.

It is not practical to list all activities or interests which might be considered to be in conflict with the interests of the Company. However, once each year for several years the attention of all managerial employees has been directed to this general subject and it is believed a clear understanding prevails as to the policy of the Company. Thus, it is considered to be in conflict with the Company's interest:

> (a) for an employee to *seek* or *accept*, or to *offer* or provide, directly or indirectly, *from* or *to* any individual, partnership, association, corporation, or other business entity or representative thereof, doing or seeking to do business with the Company or any affiliate of the Company, loans (except with banks or other financial institutions), services, payments, excessive entertainment and travel, vacation

or pleasure trips, any gift or gifts of money in any amount;

(b) for an employee to serve as an officer, director, employee or consultant of another company or organization which is a competitor of the Company or which is doing or seeking to do business with the Company or any affiliate, except that with the knowledge and consent of the President of the Company such employee may serve as a director of a corporation which is doing business with the Company, where no competitive situation is present;

(c) for an employee to use, or reveal (without proper authorization) to a third party, any confidential product information, data on decisions, plans, or any other information concerning the Company or any affiliate, which might be prejudicial to the interest of the Company or to any affiliate;

(d) for an employee or member of his immediate family to have any interest, direct or indirect, in any organization which has business dealings with the Company or any affiliate, except when such interest comprises securities in widely held corporations that are traded regularly in recognized security markets, and such interest is not in excess of 1 percent of the outstanding stock or other securities of such corporation, or except when such interest has been fully disclosed to the President of the Company for a determination as to the substantiality of such interest and the propriety of retaining it; or

(e) for an employee to use, or permit others to use, Company employees, materials, or equipment improperly for personal purposes.

Example B

1. *Policy.* It is the policy of the Company that its directors, officers, and employees shall not assume or maintain relationships or practices that inhibit or prej-

udice, in reality or by implication, the objective exercise of sound ethical business judgment, or that otherwise adversely affect the Company.

2. *The Company's Position.* The Company recognizes and respects the individual's right to engage in activities outside of his employment or association with the Company which are private in nature, or which in no way conflict with, or adversely reflect upon the Company or its image. It reserves the right, however, to determine when an individual's activities are in conflict with the Company's interests, and to take whatever action is required to remove this conflict, including, if necessary, termination of employment or association. The conduct of the individual must conform to the best interests of the Company in all cases.

3. *Standards of Business Ethics.* What constitutes a conflict of interest or an unethical practice is both a moral and legal question. It is not possible in a general policy statement to describe all circumstances and relationships that fall within this category. The following, however, suggest the types of activity which may reflect upon the personal integrity of the individual employed by, or associated with, the Company and which limit his ability ethically to discharge his responsibilities to the Company.

(a) Employment by another firm while in the employment of this Company, particularly if the firm is or would be a competitor or supplier.

(b) The holding of a substantial interest in or the participation in the management of a firm to which the Company makes sales or from which the Company makes purchases.

(c) Speculation or dealing in materials, equipment, supplies, services, or property purchased by the Company.

(d) The borrowing of money from customers or from individuals or firms from which the Company buys services, materials, equipment, or supplies or with whom the Company does business, other than recognized loan institutions.

(e) The acceptance of gifts with more than nominal value, or excessive entertainment from an outside organization or agency.

(f) The participation in civic, professional, or other organizational activities in a manner whereby confidential Company information is divulged.

(g) The misuse of privileged information or the revealing of confidential data to outsiders.

(h) The acquisition or sale of the stock of the Company, for quick profits or speculation.

(i) The carrying on of Company business with a firm in which the individual or any near relative of the individual has appreciable ownership or interest.

(j) The misuse of Company position or knowledge of Company affairs for outside gains.

(k) The acquisition of securities or other property which the Company itself has interest in acquiring.

(l) Engaging in practices or procedures which violate the anti-trust laws or other laws regulating the conduct of the Company's business.

4. *The Obligations of the Individual.*

(a) Employment by or association with the Company carries with it the responsibility to be constantly aware of the importance of ethical conduct and the requirement to be exemplary in such conduct. The individual must disqualify himself from taking part, or exerting any influence, in any transaction in which his own interests may conflict with the best interests of the Company.

(b) Interests that might otherwise be questionable may be entirely proper if accompanied by a full disclosure which affords an opportunity for prior approval or disapproval. The obligation to make such disclosure rests upon the individual.

5. *Procedure.* Any individual who is engaged in activities set forth in Section 3, or in any other activities that might represent a conflict with the Company's interests or result in interference with effective performance of his position, or who contemplates becoming so engaged, is urged to so notify the Chairman of the Board or the Corporate Director of Personnel and Public Relations as appropriate, either directly or through his Division Manager or through his Division Industrial Relations Manager so that a corporate opinion may be obtained as to the propriety of such action. Individuals who choose not to bring such activities to the attention of management shall be individually responsible for that decision.

6. *Definitions.* For the purpose of this policy the following definitions apply:

(a) *Near Relatives* are defined as spouse, parents, brothers, sisters, children, aunts and uncles, nieces and nephews, and the spouses of brothers, sisters, and children.

(b) *Stock Speculation.* Under the provisions of Section 16(b) of the Securities and Exchange Act of 1934, it is presumed that any purchase and sale or any sale and purchase of the Company's stock by officers, directors, and certain other so-called "inside" employees of the Company occurring within a period of less than six months are speculative transactions. The Company, in the absence of extenuating circumstances, will consider the time limit imposed by Section 16(b) as the *minimum standard of conduct for all employees.*

(c) *Practices or Procedures Violating the Anti-Trust Laws.* Under the anti-trust laws the Company must make its business decisions independently, and not as the result of any agreement or understanding with any of its competitors. Therefore, no individual shall enter into any understanding, agreement, plan, or scheme with any competitor in regard to prices, terms, or conditions of sale, customers' bidding practices, discounts, or territories, nor shall any individual discuss or exchange such information or other such competitive matters with any competitor. Violation of the law carries strict penalties, both for the Company and convicted individuals. Therefore, extreme care should be taken not to engage in any practice considered doubtful until the individual has made proper inquiry and has been advised that it is lawful.

7. *Interpretation.* It is difficult to define all situations exactly. So, if there are any questions at any time on present or future interpretations, you are urged to consult with this Company following the procedure outlined in Section 5 above.

Example C

Questionnaire

Name of person answering this questionnaire: _____

Division or subsidiary: _____

Position: _____

1. Do you, or to your knowledge do any members of your family, have any ownership interest in or loans from, or have you or they received any personal gain in any form from, any person or firm which does business* with——or any subsidiary

of_____? (Ownership of securities issued by such a firm and listed on a public stock exchange need not be considered in answering this question. Also gifts of nominal value for business use, such as daybooks, etc., need not be considered.)

Answer: _____

2. Would your answer to the preceding question have been "yes" at any time during the past three years?

Answer: _____

3. Do you have reason to believe that either of the preceding questions would require a "yes" answer by an employee who is under your supervision?

Answer: _____

If your answer to any of these questions is "yes," please submit a detailed explanation.

The above answers are true and correct.
Dated: _____

_____
(Signature)

_____
Notary Public

* This is intended to include any company, partnership, or individual from which_____or a subsidiary buys any product or service, or to which_____or a subsidiary sells any product or service.

ETHICAL POLICY IN PURCHASING

Example D

• All purchasing personnel will adhere to the highest standards of integrity and personal conduct and thereby maintain and promote our reputation as an outstanding company with which to do business.

• We do not take advantage of clerical error of suppliers. In practice, we expect our suppliers to reciprocate.

• We will avoid even the appearance of commercial bribery by discouraging in every way possible the presentation of gifts, tickets, or other favors. Association with suppliers' representatives at meals or other occasions is desirable when it is mutually convenient, provided we are able to act as host on occasion as well as guest.

• Under no circumstances will purchasing personnel make any purchase commitments with relatives or with sources in which the individual making the commitment has more than an incidental financial interest. In the event that the best interests of the Corporation are not served by adhering to this policy, the person involved will disqualify himself from the matter, referring it to his immediate supervisor and the concerned General Purchasing Agent.

• We will never knowingly exaggerate our requirements for the purpose of temporarily enjoying a better price. Similarly, we will never knowingly underestimate our requirements or deny the existence of a requirement simply because we prefer not to do business with a particular supplier.

• We will not misrepresent competitors' prices, quality, or services to obtain concessions.

• The Corporation subscribes to the "Principles and Standards of the National Association of Purchasing Agents."

Example E

Employees are prohibited from transacting business with any individual formerly employed by this corporation who is acting in a sales or liaison capacity as an officer, employee, agent, or representative of any supplier or prospective supplier:

(a) for a period of two years after the termination of his employment, or

(b) with respect to any specific subject matter with which he was directly connected during the period of his employment.

10 FIGURES THAT LIE

While shrinkage ranges from 1.2 percent to 5.5 percent of sales on a companywide basis, according to the National Retail Merchants' Association, some downtown stores suffer losses as high as 8 percent. Despite the widespread use of electronic devices, closed-circuit television, and plainclothes and uniformed security guards, losses remain substantial. Nevertheless, executives are very reluctant to believe that their inventory shortages are an actual dollar loss. Indeed, if merchandise stock shortages were charged to expense, instead of showing as a reduction of gross margin, it would rank as one of the largest individual expenses. By the same reasoning, if we could think of it as an expense and treat it as such, we could, I think, make the greatest possible stride toward keeping stock shortage dollars at a minimum.

A department store's inventory shortage climbs to a damaging 3.5 percent. Something is wrong—but management shrugs it off: "It must have been an inaccurate inventory. An aberration. We'll pick it up next year." Next year's shortage is an acceptable 2 percent. But the store does *not* pick up the previous year's slack. "Well, things are evening off, though . . . maybe next year. . . ." Next year the figure stays at about 2 percent. And then, in the fourth year, the establishment is clobbered with a disastrous 4 percent "shrinkage." Now they admit there is a problem; now it may be too late.

Figures can signal trouble. Shortages should obviously be looked into. Extreme fluctuations may indicate that something is wrong. But suppose the figures coming out are uniformly good? That means everything is all right, doesn't it?

No, it doesn't. There is such a thing as figures being *too* good.

The Building Equipment Company leases construction equipment and operates nationwide. Most of the better BEC agencies achieve 78 to 80 percent usage of the equipment. But for five years the Cincinnati agency had been showing a phenomenal 90 percent usage or higher. This intensity of use seemed to be matched by the bottom-line figures coming out of the operation. Headquarters had sent people down there, not because they suspected anything was wrong, but because they wanted to find out how Cincinnati did it.

The answer as to what made the Cincinnati agency so profitable remained elusive. Top management chalked it up to the immense flair for the business of the Cincinnati manager, Ted Wilson. Wilson was relatively new to the business, but he had definite ideas and impressed everyone as a go-getter. At conventions he was BEC's star performer. But there was something else about Wilson that struck the president of BEC. Wilson's salary was $24,000 a year; with bonuses he made about $30,000. Yet he lived in a house that must have cost at least $85,000. He belonged to a country club with annual dues of $4,000.

The generally accepted explanation was that Wilson, in his second marriage, had chosen a bride whose father was wealthy. The father-in-law was supposed to have paid for the house, and for many of the other amenities enjoyed by the Wilsons. Still the president wondered. One day he got to wondering hard enough to contact Norman Jaspan Associates.

We examined the same figures headquarters had examined; we found nothing unusual. We began to check further. The only odd fact that turned up was this: Wilson was the landlord for the Louisville agency. There was nothing wrong with this in itself—but the fact had never been communicated to headquarters. Why not? Our interest in Wilson intensified. We decided to watch him for a while.

BEC managers spend a lot of time out of the office, dropping around to the sites on which leased BEC equipment is at work. Wilson did visit many of the places where, on the basis of the record, there was heavy usage of BEC equipment. But he also visited *other* sites where no BEC equipment was in use, at least according to company records.

Around this time a strange thing happened. Wilson contacted headquarters: "I am beginning to wonder," he said, "whether everything is on the up-and-up in Louisville. About a year ago that agency picked up some equipment from a bankrupt company. I wonder if it has been reported. I can't find out much, and if there's nothing wrong I don't want to jeopardize my relationship with them. Why don't *you* send somebody down there to pull a surprise audit?"

Management followed through and found nothing amiss.

Another of those nagging little facts came to light in the meantime. Wilson's office had issued a W-2 form to a Fred Wilson, who turned out to be the manager's first cousin. There was a company policy against employing relatives. Exceptions had been made—but Ted Wilson had never asked for an exception.

The question was, should we confront Wilson with what we had learned so far? That is frequently one of the toughest questions to face during an investigation. If it turns out to be a false alarm, the company may have destroyed the effectiveness of a profitable operation and lost one of its best men. We decided not to take that bold step yet. Instead, we began a systematic examination of building sites within Wilson's area to see just how much BEC equipment was in operation.

And the story began to emerge. Wilson certainly had intensive usage of his equipment—much more intensive than headquarters imagined. There was a lot more BEC equipment being used in his area than the company carried on its books. Wilson had obtained the extra equipment by buying it and not reporting it, by writing off certain equipment that was still operable, and by persuading the managers of other locations (notably Louisville) to "lend" him equipment. He was leasing out at cut rates, and inducing contractors to pay him in cash. He was pocketing more than $60,000 a year, and had a number of associates on his "gravy train."

He settled for $200,000—cash—and still had enough left to move to another state and reestablish himself in business.

In retailing, also, a figure can be *too* good. Excessive shortages or unduly fluctuating figures are causes for concern. But *inventory overages* offer what amounts to prima facie evidence of manipulation. How does an inventory overage come about? Here is a typical case.

Mrs. Gallon, a buyer for a northwestern department store, had had a run of bad luck. Many of the styles she bought for the spring were dogs that did not move, and marked down, they did not move much better in the summer either. Her summer purchases also moved slowly; and fall was no improvement. Now inventory time was approaching. Mrs. Gallon knew perfectly well that the top merchandising manager, when he saw the reports, would be unhappy. He might very well fire her. So she determined to "update" her old, slow-moving stock and make it look like current season merchandise.

How could this be done? To the eye of a professional in the trade, the old coats and dresses would look exactly like what they actually were—" dogs." But the inventory was not taken by someone wise in the clothing business; it was taken by an auditor's clerk. The clerk reads tags and box labels, and enters figures on his ledger sheets. Style does not mean much to him.

Most stores use a season code on certain classifications of merchandise, notably women's wear. "W" designated the spring stock, "M" the summer stock, and "P" the more recent fall stock of Mrs. Gallon. She had practically all her "W" and "M" merchandise reticketed as "P" and marked up (unrecorded, of course) to original price for the inventory. The day after the inventory she had the designations changed back to reflect reality.

The auditor's clerk dutifully recorded what he saw on the tickets. When the merchandise manager saw the results, he must have been initially pleased. She had obviously turned over her spring and summer stock very well, since there was no evidence of old stock or drastic markdowns.

But of course when the year-end figures finally arrived, the department would show an inventory overage. Now the question is, will Mrs. Gallon get away with it? The overage should alert management to the fact that something is wrong, but that doesn't always happen. Some stores still ride along a surprising distance in the face of facts that call for action. Eventually Mrs. Gallon's pyramiding operation will topple. For she is caught in a vicious cycle. Since she has reported a min-

imum of old merchandise, she is in no position to
request widespread markdown privileges to get rid of
it. She will have to mark down drastically anyway,
without reporting it. And then the inventory shortage
figure will skyrocket.

This kind of thing would be avoided if merchandise
managers simply took an occasional walk through the
departments under their jurisdiction and looked at the
merchandise. To the practiced eye it would become
quickly apparent that the buyer was loaded with eigh-
teen-month-old stock which was being reported as
new.

The activity is fraudulent, but it is not done for
direct personal gain. The buyer is just trying to keep her
job. She knows that paper results can keep management happy for a long time.

It is not hard for basically honest employees to
justify this sort of thing. Suppose a buyer is stuck
with a lot of unsold merchandise after the Christmas
season. She says to herself: "The season was short, only
five and a half weeks. The weather was bad. The personnel department must have run a dragnet through
Skid Row to get. the extra help they gave me. Not
only do these people not know how to write up an order, they can't even ring up a cash register. Why should
I be penalized for their shortcomings?"

And so she "improves" her results, rationalizing that
they *would* have been this good if she had been given
a decent amount of support. She knows that if the merchandise manager comes through and begins comparing
tickets with the dresses on which they are hanging, she
is in deep trouble. But she also knows her merchandise
manager, and she knows he won't do that.

One vital principle of locating and stopping fraud
is: *look at the actuality first,* and then compare it with
the records that are supposed to represent actuality.

Often we take a close look at the "security" practices that management is proudest of and considers most foolproof. For example, a manufacturer of air conditioners calls us in upon learning that his units are being offered for sale by dealers who are not on the company's lists. He suspects they are counterfeits. We suggest that these air conditioners are made in the company's plant and identical with the "authorized" stock.

"But that can't be. Every unit that comes off our line is accounted for."

"Accounted for how?"

And then management proudly describes its serial-numbering system. Every unit carries a plaque with a consecutive serial number. These numbers are carefully checked. The yield of every run is recorded. And every shipment adds up before it goes out. "There is no way that units could be made without our knowing about it."

The serial number plaque is the magic protective device, just as it was for the organ company. And when management sets such store by a "fool-proof" mechanism, we concentrate on that and it usually pays off. In this case it took just a day or so—for us to locate the machine that was stamping out the *duplicate* serial number plaques.

In another example, a manufacturer of electronic equipment finds that his products are appearing on the market in greater numbers than can be accounted for. "But they must be fakes. They can't be being made here."

"Why not? Why can't somebody simply put together an extra one here and there?"

The plant manager beams. He produces a nine-inch-thick sheaf of blue papers. "These are the job tickets on *one single unit*. We go much farther than most manufacturers. We account for every nut, every wire, every terminal. A guy can't get away with a single component, let alone enough to put together an extra unit."

Again, the answer is simple. The procedure is so painstakingly detailed that it looks foolproof to management. But because it is so detailed, it cannot be fully adhered to, so supervisors take shortcuts. Workers know the shortcuts are being taken; and it is relatively easy to produce extra components, fake job tickets, and produce expensive units destined for the black market.

We take a hard look at the procedures for correcting mistakes. If they are complex and difficult, then we may be on the way to locating the source of certain "losses."

The stores in a supermarket chain had been shorted to the tune of $40,000 in thirteen weeks. The president was up in arms. He had already taken action. "We stopped thirty of our trailers on the road and unloaded them top-to-bottom right there. And sure enough, we found that a lot of the shipments were short. A tremendous number. And we want to get to the bottom of it—find out how widespread this thing is."

The president was convinced that he was being robbed by a widespread conspiracy. However, after looking over some of the chain's procedures, we were not so sure. We suggested a quick warehouse inventory. We said, "Fifty-fifty you find an *overage*."

"An overage? Impossible."

But we turned out to be right. The warehouses had more stock than the records showed they should. What was going on?

The "conspiracy" consisted of the store's own complicated methods. Here was the way the "culprit" operated: A warehouse worker has a shipping ticket to fill—say, ten cases of soup to store X. The worker can locate only seven cases of soup. But he can't just change the ticket to read seven cases instead of ten. If he does that it might mean his job. Any change in a shipping voucher requires an elaborate procedure.

So, instead, the man simply loads seven cases and sends them out, without changing the ticket. The checking procedure on the other end is loose, again because the system is so complicated. So the stores are being "shorted"; but the stock is not being stolen. It is simply never getting out of the warehouse.

One important difference between retailing and other industries lies in their relative sensitivity to inventory losses. A manufacturing firm, for example, may be suffering severe losses through fraud and pilferage and still not be aware of the problem. But retailers are keenly attuned to their vulnerability to inventory shortage. A well-run department store may show a net profit of 3 percent. At the same time, that store's inventory loss may be 2 percent. So if the establishment is doing $100 million worth of business annually, it is making $3 million—and it is losing $2 million through shortage. Moreover, this 2 percent shortage figure is likely to be regarded as "acceptable." But if it begins to move upward—2½ percent, 2¾ percent—then the entire profit is in danger of being wiped out.

There are two principal contributors to inventory shortages. One factor is out-and-out theft—removal of merchandise. This is done by outsiders, that is, shoplifters, or by the employees of the store. The other factor is procedural, resulting in "phantom" shortages. Merchandise is recorded as having been received when, in fact, it never reached the store's stockroom; or it is damaged and surreptitiously disposed of or perhaps a price-change document got lost in the paper-work shuffle.

Some of the procedural factors that contribute to inventory shortages are the result of human error. Theoretically these errors should even out. In practice, of course, they do not. The shopper will very likely correct an error that is in the store's favor, but will readily accept an error in the other direction.

As a matter of fact, studies in the supermarket industry show that only about 25 percent of all customers are charged the correct amount for their total orders. As high as 65 percent are undercharged an average of 1 percent of total sales. Less than 10 percent are overcharged.

Retail establishments are vulnerable to many sophisticated forms of fraud. One center for this kind of fraud is the receiving dock. The receiving dock of a store is a busy, and sometimes frantic place. Trucks are backing up to deliver everything from shoelaces to washing machines. Suppose a truck is unloaded, and somebody signs a receipt signifying delivery of one hundred television sets. But quite by accident, only ninety sets have been unloaded. The clerks at the receiving platform intend to check the shipment, but two more trucks have pulled up and several drivers, sweating and cursing, are waiting their turn. The count is hurried and perfunctory. Maybe no count is taken; instead the clerks accept the driver's word. So the truck driver pulls out with a receipt for a hundred sets, though he has delivered only ninety. Often no deception is intended.

But the same procedure may not be so innocent. Let's take this same driver. Once he did unload a short shipment at the XYZ Store. They signed for it. (There are dozens of such cases every day.) He noticed the error later and came back with the rest of the goods. But he decided to test the water. He made a partial delivery again; and again he got a full receipt. Now he is in business. He pulls up and sees that the receiving personnel are rushed and harried. He unloads part of his shipment—enough to look like a substantial amount—and then presents his receipt form. If somebody catches the shortage, it's a mistake. If not, the driver pulls away with his loot, and the store has a shortage. What will the driver do with the merchandise? In every city of any size there are fences who do a thriving business in goods that come onto the black market in this fashion.

The driver may continue to work this fast shuffle on his own, but sooner or later he will get caught or at least become an object of suspicion. It is much easier and more convenient for him to enter into a safe, comfortable relationship with at least one of the checkers who work on the receiving dock. He arranges to split the take. Now he can arrive at a designated time and be sure that he will get a "short count" and drive away with a signed stub. This is a common method of collusive stealing. Hundreds of drivers arrange their routing schedules to conform with the schedules of their accomplices on the platforms of various establishments. The black market receives a steady infusion of goods. Shortage percentages rise. This is *bulk* theft; it takes a lot of individual shoplifting to come even close to equaling it.

How valid a receiving record can be produced? The receiving record should truly indicate the quantity and kind of goods received. But this does not always happen. The basic principle of security in receiving goods is double accountability. The foreman on the loading dock examines and counts the merchandise and signs a record describing what has come in. Then a second, independent party verifies the count. When the goods are moved to the stockroom, but before they go into stock, somebody else countersigns to provide verification of the initial receiving record. This may be a stockroom employee or a department head.

Double accountability must be applied selectively. The store decides which articles are most prone to error, defalcation, or diversion. Obviously you start with movie projectors, TV sets, fur coats, men's suits; you may be willing to take your chances with cashew nuts and paper napkins. Double-check the merchandise that is most desirable to thieves and that costs you the most.

As vulnerable as retail establishments may appear, the losses sustained by manufacturing companies are even greater, but these losses are not as conspicuous because they are masked by their methods of accounting.

In industry, one of the situations most open to major fraud is construction—let's say the building of an addition or a new plant. Here we are dealing with *services* as well as with measurable things—contractors' bills for materials, for labor, and for rental of equipment. And this rental can be huge. A single massive construction machine may rent for $500 a day. The construction site, to the uninitiated eye, is a seething mass of men and machines. Who can make heads or tails out of it?

Given this situation, it is inevitable that we have seen a great boom in padded contractors' bills. Suppose a contractor's bill states that six earth movers were in use for five days. The customer doesn't know whether all the earth movers were in operation for the full five days. A subcontractor submits an invoice for fifty tons of pipe. The pipe was delivered in the middle of the night, and anyway much of it has now been used. Were there really fifty tons in the initial shipment, or only forty? The customer can be at the mercy of the contractor on materials and rentals.

The key to this situation is the customer's project engineer. This individual must be able to devote full time and energy to the policing of the construction contract, and he must have sufficient people. In essence, it is a continuing verifying procedure. A man is assigned to count the number of trench-digging machines at work on a given day. He must list the machines by number. He must make sure they are actually at work, not left on the site until the contractor needs them elsewhere, a common practice. The project engineer must see to it that the "midnight delivery" is verified for full count or, indeed, that the shipment was made at all.

Too often the person designated as project engineer may not know too much about what the contractor is really doing. He is likely to be trying to split his time between ongoing duties and the "extra" assignment. So when an inflated contractor's bill comes in, he may be suspicious, but not have the facts or the experience to go beyond suspicion. So he approves all documents without question. Thus, every day industry is billed for machines that did not operate, men who did not work, material that was never received.

Of course the best way for the builder to avoid all this is to award a flat-price contract. Why isn't this done more often? For one thing, there is the vital matter of time. Contractors don't like flat-payment deals (many refuse them altogether). They must figure very closely in estimating their bids on such work. The builder must work hard to make every specification exact. This process can take weeks, or months, and the builder can't afford to wait that long. So he takes his chances on being billed on the notorious cost-plus basis.

So in the end it comes down to a project engineer. And even if he is knowledgeable and adequately supported, the customer is still not out of the woods. There is the ever-present possibility of collusion between the engineer (or members of his staff) and the contractor.

11 HOW TO GUARD TRADE SECRETS

The headlines of the early 1970s have made us all conscious of the problem of security of information: the Pentagon Papers, Watergate, and so on. Most companies possess information that must be kept secret. There are, or should be, degrees of classification: Top Secret, Confidential, and so forth. Such information comprises P & L statements, market reports, yield statistics, formulas, research reports—anything that should not fall into unauthorized hands.

The information may be in files, blueprints, computer printouts, or it may be on magnetic tape. As the technological means of generating information have made quantum jumps, the difficulties of protecting information have proliferated. The quick-copying machine has made a joke of many previously effective security measures. The new industry of data communication is creating serious headaches for businessmen and security professionals, who ask themselves how the data communicated can be protected. As of now, industry experts confess they have no easy answers.

The tougher you make it to retrieve information, by lockup or by restricted access, the harder you make it for yourself to do business. Many people must have certain information to do their jobs. Many other people *think* they need the information, and are highly insulted when it is kept from them.

It's easy to run off duplicate tapes—mailing lists, for example. Many companies place complete responsibility for protecting such sensitive material in the hands of the data processing manager. But this arrangement frequently does not work. The EDP man is hardware-oriented. He is an expert on computers, but one reel of tape may be much like another to him. His orientation toward the bread-and-butter needs of the business may be very slight. This is not the man to protect highly classified reels of magnetic tape. Besides that, most large computer installations run twenty-four hours a day, seven days a week. The economics of computers dictates this setup. The manager can't be on hand all the time; subordinate personnel will frequently be in charge. What is to prevent the man working, say, the Sunday graveyard shift, from running off the prime list and selling it to a willing competitor? One common-sense answer to the question is to be extremely reluctant to classify anything. Place the "Secret" label on only the most absolutely sensitive material and then subject this handful of material to the most rigorous safeguards: locked vault, guards, the works. All other information could be protected by reasonable measures.

Recent court decisions relative to the theft of company secrets underscore the importance of this common-sense approach.

Most of our cases of theft of trade secrets begin with a suspicion. Our first task is to bring insight and experience to bear on that suspicion, to dispel it or to substantiate it with hard facts. Our second task is to recommend and establish policies, procedures, controls, and training programs that will result in a better-run company.

A lot of cases start with a phone call: One such came from the president of Pasteur Laboratories. He had an odd incident to relate. Pasteur was then involved in a $35-million expansion involving additions and new plants across the United States. Much of this expansion had been made necessary by some new and highly confidential processes Pasteur had developed. Paul Mason, the chief architect, told Pasteur's president this story: About six weeks before, Mason got a call from a mutual friend who wanted him to meet with a Mr. Henry to discuss a business proposition. Mason met with Henry. After some general preliminaries, Henry said, "I hear you are doing some work for Pasteur Laboratories." And then the purpose of the call was revealed. Henry would like a tour of the new plant. He offered Mason a $10,000 retainer and an additional $50,000 fee upon delivery of a full set of plans. Mason said Henry seemed to know that Mason would not have a problem inviting him or his associates into the plant—that if they went in with Mason, who could supply them with the type of hard hats used in the plant, everyone would assume that they were part of Mason's crew and would not question them. Mason told the president that he waited six weeks to tell him about this approach, hoping that he would have more concrete information, and that he consented to the fee only as a ruse to draw Henry out to see what he was really aiming at. Mason was a sophisticated man. He had been around. Why six weeks?

The more we thought about it, the more we were concerned about Mason's delay in reporting to management. With this in mind, we decided to talk to three young project engineers who had worked with the architect without disclosing the purpose of the conversation. As we spoke with each one separately, we became certain that the architect was actively seeking out confidential information. It was much too coincidental that his conversations with the engineers took place in the last couple of weeks, and that all centered around the new processes.

None of the engineers was aware of the fact that he was really involving the architect or himself. The three engineers ultimately confessed: It was their responsibility to determine production methods, and select and recommend the equipment that was to be utilized. All of the competing firms entertained them lavishly, but one outdid the others. They were picked up in a private plane and taken to inspect its plant on the coast. Instead of going directly to the plant, they stopped off in Las Vegas for a luxurious, expense-paid, long weekend, and each was furnished with a thousand dollars worth of chips, through the courtesy of this company. Of course, its plans were accepted.

The disclosures of the three men were merely side-effects of the investigation. This happens in a surprising number of cases. We go into an organization to investigate a certain condition or suspected problem. We talk with people. And altogether unrelated problems and defalcations begin to emerge—frequently as "windfall" confessions. The employee with a guilty secret assumes that he is the target, when in fact he has been approached only to elicit background information.

We realized the project's entire engineering operation should be examined closely, but we still hadn't resolved the mystery of Henry's and Mason's relationship.

The question to decide now was, should we talk with Mason or with Henry? We chose Henry because the research we had undertaken disclosed, among other things, that Henry was actually named Hennessy, and was vice-president in charge of professional placement at Extra Help, Inc.

An associate and I dropped into the executive offices of Extra Help, Inc., one morning, told the receptionist that we had no appointment, and asked if Hennessy was available. She escorted us into his office. At first, Hennessy was cordial and pleasant and even offered us coffee. Although we did not tell him all the details, we hinted about a new construction site concerning which he might be of assistance. His personality changed sharply: "I'm sorry gentlemen, I don't understand what you are talking about. I'm sorry I can't help you. Good day."

We made a pretext of leaving, and then as if as an afterthought, asked if we could see the president. Hennessy left the office and was back a few minutes later: "I'm sorry, the president won't be back until this afternoon."

"Okay. What about seeing your house counsel?"

With this, he made a brief, noncommittal call, and then told us the attorney would not be in until late afternoon. We mentioned that we had traveled over 200 miles that morning, that it was raining, and that we had no place to go. Since he had so many interviewing offices, we asked if we could have the use of one until either the president or their attorney came in. Reluctantly, he obliged, but his anger and the pressure were beginning to show.

There was always a possibility that we had made an error and that perhaps he was not the right man. Although we were 95 percent certain, we wanted to be 100 percent positive. That one chance in a thousand that there was a slipup somewhere can occur, but one must take precautions that it will not happen no matter how solid the case looks.

Hennessy left us, mumbling that he had to make an important call to Europe and we had already delayed him. We felt it was an important call, all right, but not to Europe. If he were the guilty person, he probably wanted to call the architect and a few other people to find out where they had slipped. This was probably the most revealing aspect of the morning. We sensed his tension in his statement regarding the urgency of the phone call.

An hour later Hennessy came barging into the office with his topcoat and said, "Let's get out of here and have lunch some place where we can talk." Now, he seemed more frustrated than before, and we felt the purpose of the invitation was not to reveal anything to us, but to find out what we knew.

After his second drink he relaxed a bit and, finally, told us the following: He used to be a chemical engineer and worked for a chemical construction company before accepting his present position, where, for the past four years, he had been earning $50,000 a year. He still did consulting on the outside; at any rate, he picked up good leads from time to time that he referred to his old boss; this was giving him additional income.

He indicated he had a large following among professional people, and that he was responsible for bringing into Extra Help, Inc., the temporary professional help division—chemists, engineers, architects, etc. And it would not be unusual for him to pick up some promising leads and, perhaps, even some processes and methods that could be useful to his old clients or potential clients. He asserted that he saw nothing wrong in this because if he wanted to, and had the time, there was no plant he could not penetrate one way or another. Since he did not have the time, he said, "I had to resort to some of my outside contacts in this case."

We explained: "I'm sure by now you realize that you used bad judgment and may have jeopardized your future and the reputation of your company. You may even force government regulation upon the whole billion-dollar temporary help industry in order to provide the innocent employer some legal protection. If what you are doing prevails in your industry, the temporary professional help working in contract engineering firms, banks, research and development departments in practically any company can walk away with the whole business . . . so the problem goes far beyond your involvement.

"Now, let's get down to business. We did our homework thoroughly. We understand how these situations can come about, but that does not make it right. We would like to go back to the board of directors and inform them that you were cooperative and made a full disclosure including the name of the competitor who sought the information."

He replied: "I don't know the name of the competitor. I was working through my old boss on the coast. That's all I know."

We suggested that he think about it and give us a call between 10:00 and 11:00 A.M. the next day if he cared to discuss the matter further. If not, we would be obliged to present the facts, as we knew them, to our client's legal department. We concluded, "Now let's eat our lunch." At this, Hennessy said, "I've lost my appetite," and ordered another brandy.

Promptly at 10:00 A.M. the next day the chief counsel for our client received a call. It was from the head of the legal department of one of their main competitors. The caller got to the point: "It has come to our attention that one of our overeager junior executives may have been a bit too zealous in trying to find out as much as he could about the competition. We are sorry for any misunderstading that may have resulted from a perfectly natural and innocent mistake. . . ."

Of course, the story does not end there. As a matter of fact, it is far from over as this is written. But now

Pasteur Laboratories *knows* who wanted the plans for the new processes. Pasteur now is taking the necessary steps to protect itself legally.

This story illustrates some of the principles of our business:

Don't take anything for granted. Pasteur's president was alert enough to realize that this was a matter that merited investigation. He was not willing to take the architect's vague explanation for his delay at face value, and his sensitivity to the potential ramifications impelled him to seek professional advice.

Look for the windfalls. Very few companies suffer from just one isolated problem of fraud. An investigation will usually turn up leads on unrelated matters which may turn out to be as important as the original lead.

Be patient. Don't automatically take the most obvious and direct approach. You can alert everyone involved and blow the whole investigation. Work around the periphery of the problem first and stay with each phase until it is resolved.

Always look for the positive lessons that can be learned. During a discussion of the problem of security, one Pasteur executive exclaimed: "My God! What about the plant we built in Memphis four years ago? One of the vendors on that job wanted some on-site photos for his promotion brochure. I told him he could take them." From this emerged a general policy about not permitting visits by outsiders to potentially sensitive areas. The theft of company secrets has been accelerating with such rapidity and is so widespread that a complacent management can find itself with no business to manage if proper safeguards are not taken. Fortunately, the judicial test of a trade secret hinges on the measures taken by a company to protect its privileged material from outside disclosure. Thus, if reasonable steps are taken to protect a company's trade secrets, then the courts will generally rule in favor of the injured party.

Judge Irving L. Goldberg of the U.S. Circuit Court of Appeals at New Orleans handed down a landmark decision on corporate spying in which aerial photography was involved. The litigation pertained to a multi-million dollar methanol manufacturing plant that was being built by the Du Pont Company in Beaumont, Texas. Methanol is used to manufacture anti-freeze by an unpatented process. The photographer admitted in court that he took the aerial photos for delivery to another party, but he claimed that he was violating no laws in doing so.

Judge Goldberg's decision was influenced by the measures that had been taken by Du Pont to protect the secrecy of the production process. The judge observed that although there was no fraud or trespass, the defendant's rights had been violated. He commented: "Our devotion to freewheeling industrial competition must not force us into accepting the law of the jungle as the standard of morality expected in our commercial relations. . . . One may use his competitor's secret process if he discovers it by reverse engineering applied to the finished product, or if he discovers it by his own independent research; but one may not avoid these labors by taking the process from the discoverer without his permission at a time when he is taking reasonable precautions to maintain its secrecy."

The recent award of $21.9 million to the International Business Machines Corporation by Judge A. Sherman Christensen, in which he found that the Telex Corporation had infringed I.B.M. manuals that had been copyrighted, and had hired I.B.M. personnel for the purpose of gaining trade secrets from them, underscores the magnitude of some of these losses. (Of course, the award to I.B.M. is more than balanced by the huge damages assessed against I.B.M. for anti-competitive measures against Telex.) The very high cost of research and development in chemical, electronics, and other technologically oriented industries makes them particularly vulnerable to industrial espionage by their competitors who want to capitalize on their successes, without risking any of their own funds on research.

The prevalent tendency of companies to put many of their corporate secrets into a computer facilitates misappropriation when inadequate measures are taken to protect information stored on reels or discs in the tape library or in the computer itself. Moreover, loyalty to a corporation has often been undermined by the high degree of executive mobility that characterizes many industries.

Experience has shown that those engaged in industrial espionage may be either employees or outsiders. An employee may be anyone from a librarian to an executive; he may be a disgruntled scientist who feels no particular loyalty to his employer, or a disappointed manager inherited as the result of a merger. The outsider is usually a professional in appropriating trade secrets: He may come in as a job applicant who elicits from the personnel department highly confidential information, or a writer who ostensibly is doing an in-depth story on the company's activities, or a person with an engineering degree who arranges to be employed as a porter on a night cleaning crew provided by an outside service.

Controls that electronics companies and chemical producers set up to protect themselves from loss of trade secrets are, in some cases, far less stringent than precautions taken in the toy industry. One president of a toy design concern cites the following protective steps for his firm:

• No toy designs go out for blueprinting; new toys are referred to by numbers, not by names.
• Each night rough models and prototypes of toys under development are locked in the company vault.
• For his first six months a new employee works only on parts of toys; he is not told the purpose of the parts. Before he starts work, a new employee signs an agreement not to talk to anyone outside the firm, including his wife and children, about the toys he is working on.

One consumer-goods company had worked for a long time to develop a top-value product for which it expected a big demand. But after its researchers had finally mastered the technology involved, top management suddenly decided to shelve the item for a while because the company was busy with other top-priority production. Only eight of the company's top executives knew of that decision. Yet the very next day the president received a telephone call from the marketing manager of a company in a related field. "I understand," said the caller, "that you have postponed marketing your new product. We're disappointed, because we had hoped we could arrange some kind of tie-in sale."

How could the news have leaked out so quickly? When we visited the president's office, we observed his desk littered with confidential information.

"What do you do with all these papers at night?" we asked.

"My secretary always puts them inside my desk and locks it."

"And what does she do with the key?"

"She locks it up inside her own desk."

"All right. But then what does she do with the key to her desk?"

"Oh," said the secretary helpfully, "I put it right under this candy jar—in case someone needs it in a hurry."

If a company is worried principally about bugging devices, it can ask for a so-called electronic sweep. The experts check the telephone, the pictures, the light switches, the drapes, the rug, and the furniture—anywhere that a bug may be hidden.

Of course, as one expert points out, all that debugging can prove, no matter how thorough, is that no recording or transmitting device is operating at a given time. The next day—or the next hour, if the spy has ready access to the room—can tell a different story. There is no such thing, every expert agrees, as *permanent* debugging. It is for this reason that one New York City counterespionage firm rents limousines by the hour for top-secret executive conferences. It guarantees that they are bugproof by keeping debuggers going constantly as the limousines trundle around the city streets while the executives transact their business.

Yet those who make a living from spying and counterspying insist that the James Bond aspects of the business, because they are the most dramatic, have been overplayed, thus needlessly upsetting many businessmen. Clearly, some companies worry too much about bugs. Since there is no such thing as total security, there is no sense becoming a nervous wreck trying to achieve it. It's better to take all reasonable precautions, but not to go so far overboard that you have little energy left to apply to your own business.

There was a time, fortunately many decades ago,

when the question of an employee's privacy was a simple matter. He had none. Nor, so far as his employer was concerned, was he entitled to any private life. If the worker did not live, or think, or worship, or vote in the manner that the boss approved, he might be out of a job. A man had to do more than perform while he was on the job; he had to "measure up" during the time that he was away from the job.

We have come to agree with the principle that what the employee does with his spare time is his own business—with one important proviso: If what he does *off* the job adversely affects his performance *on* the job, or if his free-time activities are distinctly harmful to the organization, then the situation may merit concern from the employer's point of view. But even this is an extremely sensitive area. In the early days of the century George Horace Lorimer, the great editor of *The Saturday Evening Post,* is said to have expressed an attitude that has been usefully adopted by many bosses. *The Saturday Evening Post* was running a serial which at the end of a certain installment depicted the heroine as having dinner with a man. At the beginning of the next installment she is discovered having breakfast with the same man.

Well! Inasmuch as *The Saturday Evening Post* was considered to be a staunch upholder of all that was good and virtuous, segments of the magazine's readership erupted. The mail poured in to *Post* headquarters: What could the editor be *thinking* of to have permitted such unseemly comportment between his covers? In response to the onslaught, George Harris Lorimer declared, *"The Saturday Evening Post* is not responsible for what happens to its character between installments."

Managers must accept the view that the employee's time "between installments" is his own—difficult as it sometimes is to accept this view. The worker may engage in uncongenial political activity; he may drink a lot; he may be seeing, in an overly-friendly fashion, a lady other than his wife. It is his business.

His business, that is, unless and until the off-time activity begins to show adverse work-connected results. When a man is intoxicated during the working day, or so befuddled by a hangover that he cannot perform up to standard, then the boss begins to worry about it— and properly so. And if the employee spends lunchtimes or evenings disclosing to outsiders information that the organization deems confidential, then clearly his behavior somehow must be changed. However, even when such things are happening, the manager, when he confronts his subordinate, will handle the situation best if he confines his criticism to the job effects and steers clear of moralizing about how the worker should live his life.

People need time to themselves—to relax a moment, think, complain if they have a mind to. They need such time on the job as well as off. So affording employees a full measure of dignity and freedom is not only the decent thing to do. . . . it is sound and sensible management.

This is not the same thing as saying that the business-man should take no precautions whatsoever. Men *are* fallible; no cogent philosophy holds otherwise. Jean Jacques Rousseau's "natural man"—the "noble savage" —has been corrupted, in the philosopher's view, by progress in the arts and sciences.

A worker who steals violates the rights of his employer. A dishonest worker cannot draw about himself the cloak of human right to dignity merely to escape the consequences of his actions. But how can the employer prevent dishonesty or detect it without taking constructive measures?

The kind of measures that we recommend involves

checking only on what employees do or fail to do as part of their work routine. It involves scrutiny, not of the man himself, but of the job he is doing. And if all work of a given kind is reviewed according to the same standards, we can see nothing that transgresses the bounds of honorable dealings between people.

When an employer puts a fence around a building, mounts guards, even stations police dogs, is he engaging in a paranoic display of distrust and hostility against those inside and outside of his organization? Of course not. We might feel that some measures of this nature are not very effective—sometimes doing more harm than good—but they are well within the employer's right.

The fence and the burglar alarm are generic examples of two classes of preventive and detective measures which every businessman is entitled to use to safeguard his assets. They stand as symbols of passive prevention devices which, by their presence, discourage attempts at dishonesty and offer resistance to such attempts when they are made. Dual accountability of the receiving function, sound inventory-taking procedures, and confirmation of accounts are also appropriate measures for measuring performance, ascertaining accuracy, and protecting against fraud and theft of company secrets. It can be reasonably assumed that one of the social conditions of life in our form of civilization is that individuals are employed and paid by other individuals in a mutual contract and that under the contract the employee assumes certain obligations, both specified and implied. It would be hard to deny that one of these obligations is that the worker refrain from taking from his employer what he is not entitled to take—whether it be time, goods, or money.

This being so, then we must consider that the violation of that obligation carries certain sanctions. A

man cannot steal from his employer with impunity.
But if the employer is impeded in taking reasonable
precautions to prevent theft or in catching the thief,
then in practice we would find that impunity is con-
ferred upon the thief.

Where the protection of company secrets is concerned, employee rules must be fairly set, simply
presented, impartially enforced, and strictly adhered
to. The following concepts can be used as a guideline.

THE EMPLOYEE'S RESPONSIBILITY

1. The books and records of a company be-
long to the employer. An employee who removes them, secretly or openly, has violated
his legal obligations.
2. The data, information, charts, lists, and
other things directly concerned with the performance of the duties of an employee are the
property of the employer.
3. No employee can secretly deal with his
own company. Nor can he have an undis-
closed interest in a supplier firm. Nor can he
take a kickback, commission, or any other
secret profit.
4. An employee is not permitted to work for a
competitor on the sly. He cannot take a
second job with one. Any contemplated
second job with a competitor, or customer,
must be disclosed to the employer.
5. Management cannot close its eyes and ears
as to how business is generated. It is responsible for the authorized acts of its employees.
Conversely, price quotations and samples for
goods and services purchased should be a
matter of record—readily available to examination and study by higher-ups.

12 SICK HOSPITALS

To demonstrate the variety of ways in which employee dishonesty can take place, let's take a hard look at one of the most vulnerable of institutions—the hospital. Drawing on our experience, we can paint the picture of what is happening in many hospitals and health centers around the world. Then we can talk about positive solutions. The recommendations we make will show, to some extent, how we go about the task of building up methods of management that minimize opportunity and create an atmosphere of honesty.

The average American can no longer afford to get sick. The cost of treatment for serious illness is escalating at a dizzying rate, and hospitalization and medical care plans, both public and private, are proving increasingly inadequate to handle the load. In view of the fact that medical costs are one of the fastest rising components in the Cost of Living Index, the lessons to be learned can be of benefit to all of us—as patients, as taxpayers, and as participants in health insurance programs, which take more and more out of our pockets every day. So we know that illness may well lead to financial ruin; but of course human beings cannot avoid sickness by an act of the will. In fact, worries about potential medical expenses make many people sicker. This is a kind of variation on the recently developed concept of "iatrogenic intervention"—the idea that the physician's efforts to heal a patient may leave that patient in worse shape than before. Also the specter of immense hospital and medical bills can make a man sick *before* he calls for the doctor.

Of course, the crisis in health-care costs are attributable in part to general economic factors. But there is another factor that exacerbates the situation. Hospital expenses are being unhealthily inflated by an epidemic of dishonesty and waste.

Hospitals are prime targets for theft. They have cash receipts, payables, and on payday, payroll on hand. In addition there are enormous amounts of supplies, including drugs, that draw potential criminals as the pole does a compass needle. And more important than the constant possibility of theft by intruders is the threat of internal dishonesty. Tremendous quantities of vitamins, hormones, antibiotics, disposables—along with huge amounts of such items as linens and food—are purchased on a continuing basis. Control is difficult, and most inventory controls existing in hospitals today are not too formidable to the pilferer or thief who possesses a little adroitness and determination. Add to these facts the presence of expensive and easily portable office and medical equipment, often in only casually protected locations, and we begin to see the magnitude of the problem.

Bellevue Hospital in New York is a complex of thirteen buildings, honeycombed and connected by dozens of winding corridors. Every day approximately 10,000 people pass through these corridors, or loiter there. They comprise doctors, patients, hospital personnel, visitors, outside service people, and too many suspicious loungers, drug addicts, and professional thieves. Such items as dictating machines, typewriters, and adding machines are constantly disappearing. The guards who do patrol the hospital have been intimidated, threatened, and physically assaulted.

The director knows what he is up against. There are numerous entrances, many places where people can walk or hang around without being observed or questioned. And automatic elevators make it easy for anyone to go to any floor anytime. New locks have been installed on some of the more sensitive doors, but not all of them work. The outpatient department methadone center brings in addicts through any one of six doorways. Some of these patients receive treatment and then leave. Others wander, aimlessly or purposefully, through the unguarded halls. It is a security man's nightmare. As the executive director puts it: "What can you do? When 10,000 people pass through the corridors every day, how can you have effective controls? How do you watch who's coming through the door when you have one hundred and six doors?" Of course Bellevue is a public facility. But the same set of circumstances exists in just about any hospital or nursing home, public or private, of any size.

The total capital investment of all U.S. hospitals today is in excess of $30 billion. It is our third largest industry, surpassing the investment in automobile plants, railroads, and even telephone communications. A hospital comprises the operation of a pharmacy, hotel, restaurant, laundry, warehouse, research and educational institutions. And the hospital director must run all of these enterprises at the same time that he is acting as fund-raiser, educator, and public servant. He must do this with a staff that may contain a sizable percentage of high-risk personnel. In addition, the administrator must answer to both medical and lay boards, set up plans and budgets, oversee a vast purchasing mechanism, and be responsible for hundreds of details around the clock 365 days a year.

If board members who have businesses of their own tried to operate their enterprises under the same limitations imposed on the administrator, they would soon be forced to merge, sell out, or liquidate.

Take, for example, a 500-bed hospital where there are approximately three employees for every bed, plus doctors, staff, and visitors; a minimum of 3,000 to 4,000 meals a day may be served, a volume that is matched only by the largest hotels and restaurants. There is great latitude for internal theft. This was certainly the case some time ago when we were consulted about the situation at a medical center in the Midwest, where the cost of feeding patients had gone up sizably in a relatively short time, for no apparent reason. We found that the director of food services had been the beneficiary of favors and kickbacks from vendors, adding up to $25,000 within the year. Under the obligations set up by these relationships, he was overlooking flagrant and systematic padding of bills.

In the average business concern it is possible to isolate the points of greatest sensitivity, those areas where cash, equipment, or merchandise are accessible, or where dishonest employees have the chance to play with figures. But a hospital is one great area of sensitivity. For instance, in hospital after hospital a considerable number of employees augment their wages by taking home food at the institution's expense. They simply fill a shopping bag with whatever edibles happen to be around that day. Also, their households need blankets, sheets, pillow cases, and towels. These too are easily preempted. (As an interesting sidelight, we have frequently found that hospital employees, *after* stealing the linen, bring it back regularly to have it cleaned in the hospital's laundry.) These practices are not even considered stealing; many people who work in hospitals have come to think of this as merely a fringe benefit. Meanwhile, the hospital's purchases of these items go far beyond actual usage.

Of course, cash is even more useful than food or linen. In one typical case, we found that a long-time cashier in an outpatient department, well-known for her meticulous attention to detail in billing, was equally methodical in defrauding the institution. Each day she slipped into her purse the first $100 collected—no more, no less.

In another hospital the maintenance supervisor was responsible for all contract work performed on the premises by outside contractors. Our inspection of the budgets allotted for contract work over a period of years disclosed excessive labor rates and material costs. One study showed that if the painting jobs had been performed by hospital employees instead of contractors, the annual cost would have been cut in half.

Our fact-finding efforts soon disclosed the reason behind the high costs. The maintenance supervisor had his home painted at two-year intervals by obliging contractors whose heavily padded fees for hospital work more than covered the cost. Plumbing, heating, landscaping, and air-conditioning contractors willingly reciprocated in the same way.

The easiest and fastest place to cut costs is the maintenance department. Many maintenance people can be found on the job only when they are working on time and a half or double time.

At one hospital in the South, when a cold spell hit the area it was difficult to find a maintenance man on the premises. Most of them were working away from the hospital repairing or installing home heating for hospital personnel.

The pharmacy is a particularly vulnerable spot in a hospital. Control procedures are complicated by the free flow of sample merchandise and returned items.

"Give me three more years at this job," a hospital pharmacist boasted recently, "and I'll be able to retire and live out the rest of my life in luxury." This man's age was forty-two. Approximately two-thirds of his rather substantial income had been tax-free, since he naturally did not report his thefts. Our performance audit revealed he was in collusion with employees of several drug wholesalers. It was this man's practice to fill orders for his contacts in the trade by purchasing excessive quantities of drugs. These he would hand over to accomplices who made their pickups at the hospital. Cash rarely changed hands. In most instances a barter arrangement was made. These "trade agreements" involved a $4,000 sports car, a paid vacation, a handsome fur coat, a color TV set, gift certificates from fashionable stores, and other expensive items.

The pharmacist's "silent partnership" in the hospital operation was eventually uncovered when he carelessly handed a carton of drugs to one of his subordinates, instructing him to deliver it "to the man waiting in the blue Caddy in front of the hospital." The subordinate was happy to oblige. He was one of our fact-finding specialists who had been assigned the task of determining why the pharmacy costs in that particular hospital were inordinately high.

In another case a hospital pharmacist with twenty-five years' seniority acknowledged that for many years he operated his own business on the hospital premises during business hours. His inventory consisted of drugs appropriated from hospital stock as well as items obtained from detail men who were only too happy to furnish him with ample supplies of merchandise, some of which was obsolete. He would also retain samples intended for doctors, which he distributed to his own private accounts at a handsome profit.

His spouse, who was not a pharmacist, would take

instructions from her husband over the telephone and fill prescriptions from her kitchen for the neighborhood trade that could not wait for him to come home. On some items the volume dispensed by this husband-and-wife merchandising team surpassed that of the corner drugstore.

When helping himself to whatever he needed from the hospital supplies, the pharmacist rationalized that he was not being dishonest because the next time the detail man called he would ask for extra merchandise to replenish the depleted inventory. On those occasions when he did return stock, it was not necessarily the same items taken but anything he could obtain in abundance, much of it outdated and unsaleable goods.

It is not unusual for hospitals to lend drugs to neighborhood drugstores for emergency purposes. It is also not uncommon for hospital pharmacists to work as relief pharmacists in various drugstores. In many cases, the owner of the pharmacy runs short or finds it hard to get antibiotics, vaccines, or other drugs because of a scarcity. The relief pharmacist then offers to obtain it from his hospital, since hospitals always receive priority from the distributors. Upon removing it from the hospital, he makes an informal or mental note of what he is removing. When the local pharmacist replenishes his supply from his wholesaler, the drugs may be returned in a similarly informal manner, if at all.

In one such case, a hospital pharmacist's assistant had aspirations of becoming a doctor; this young man harbored the belief that the hospital should finance his medical education.

The assistant's salary was $190 per week. In his time off he was employed as a relief pharmacist in a drugstore three blocks from the hospital. The institution unwittingly competed with the wholesaler to keep the store supplied with merchandise, and thereby generously supplemented the young man's income. He stole drugs in wholesale lots, inflated breakage records, and appropriated samples and floor returns at will. He went so far as to charge narcotics and other drugs to recently expired patients, keeping the merchandise for his private use. This enterprising youth was able not only to furnish his part-time employer with needed items but to operate a sideline filling prescriptions for relatives and friends.

Professional people working in other areas also exploit their opportunities. A chief radiologist, attempting to control run-away costs, issued a memo to all doctors concerning excessive usage of X-ray film. Unfortunately, the doctors and patients were the scapegoats. The chief radiologist was not aware that two of the X-ray technicians were stealing film and selling it on a systematic basis to a private hospital. They even had the nerve to use the hospital courier service to deliver it.

A biochemist in charge of a hospital laboratory had been highly respected by the administrator and in particular by the surgeons for many years. He would become highly disturbed if his help did not show up or if he was shorthanded, particularly on the second or third shift. He took great pride in making sure that all the patients' tests were completed prior to surgery. Many times he stayed for the second and third shifts without asking for additional days off or compensation.

We became aware of this while we were performing an inventory of exposure study of the hospital's vulnerable assets. Eventually, the reason for this conscientiousness became obvious. He was in business for himself; he had been running his own medical laboratory for many years. Many of the hospital's doctors had him on a monthly retainer. He had ads under his trade name in many publications, including the Yellow Pages.

What better place could he operate from than his own little empire with all the facilities, apparatus, and a clientele which included the doctors' private patients.

During a discussion with one doctor we called to his attention that it was against hospital policy for staff members to use or hire away any personnel of the hospital to do work involving their private patients, that it would be a violation of the bylaws. His comment was that the biochemist was told to do the work only in his spare time. The doctor's concluding remark is significant: "I do not need the results immediately, since I have already treated the patients. Sometimes I wait as much as a month for the results. I just need the official reports for billing purposes."

It is one thing to announce operating rules and procedures, but quite another to enforce them and make certain they are properly understood and respected. An effective communications network designed to test performance at all levels is especially vital. This implies a periodic feedback of information to administrative personnel to determine the extent of conformity.

In the central surgical supply department, regulations specified that standard items such as syringes and surgical trays should be replenished according to a set schedule. To order other items, a formal requisition was required. At the outset the requisitioning requirement was adhered to. Then, as ward personnel became chummy with central supply employees, the system broke down and supplies were freely dispensed. The result: some of the orderlies went into business for themselves. They hoarded surgical supplies in broom closets, linen hampers, and surplus autoclaves. Arrangements were made for their contacts to enter the hospital under the guise of visitors to remove the merchandise. Many of them wore doctors' smocks that had been stolen from the laundry. So attired, they had the run of the hospital. In the evenings they were able to utilize some of the private offices to complete their transactions more efficiently.

Many of the security problems which we have illustrated can be curtailed through appropriate attention at the blueprint stage of construction. If management waits until after the building is erected, expanded, or renovated, additional expenses will be incurred in order to belatedly install safeguards which often are poor compromises.

Here are five aspects meriting attention:

1. Procedures governing the flow of food, drugs, supplies, and equipment, from time of purchase until their receipt, as well as their storage and issuance.

2. Total hospital site. The problems of perimeter security, visitors, and pedestrian and vehicular traffic; the safety of patients, visitors, and employees.

3. Accountability of cash payments, accounts receivable, and other valuables.

4. Maintaining the confidentiality of medical records and other private information.

5. Guard coverage and technology necessary for guards to perform optimally.

An effective preventive management program will aim at achieving the highest attainable level of protection of supplies and equipment, as well as of the persons and belongings of patients and employees, without adversely affecting efficiency and control. Of course, the practicality of all physical and procedural regulations has to be measured by their enforcibility. Any control measures and operating rules that require an enormous supervisory effort to enforce, or that incur deep patient and visitor resentment or high employee turnover, are bound to be ineffective.

The program has to aim at curtailment of fradulent

diversion. This includes two major categories of theft: (1) pilferage by employees, patients, and visitors and (2) large-scale diversion through collusive effort, such as between drivers and receivers, maintenance men and outside contractors, laundry workers and outsiders, professional personnel and suppliers, to name but a few examples. It must be based on an awareness of the relative risks and potential losses in both types of diversion.

Flow of Traffic

It is very difficult to curtail traffic through the corridors where patients, visitors, doctors, contractors, and employees of all levels are virtually indistinguishable. Consequently, the primary aim should be to limit the exposure of supplies and equipment, whether in storage, transit, or use.

It is important to prevent unauthorized traffic through selective areas such as the pharmacy, laboratories, central supply, or medical records library.

The question of exposure of items is directly related to the problem of space utilization. For maximum transit security, consideration must be given to vertical and horizontal transportation, including material-handling procedures, the type of conveyances used, and the required corridor dimensions and elevator facilities.

Receiving Dock

The receiving dock is a vulnerable area for large-scale diversion. The best security is to provide a receiving dock exclusively for incoming supplies and equipment.

Space and budgets permitting, there should be a separate dock for outgoing soiled and incoming fresh linen (unless the hospital has its own laundry within the complex). A separate dock for trash removal should also be provided, for both security as well as hygienic considerations. There should also be a separate loading area for the morgue.

The receiving dock should be located so as to preclude pedestrian traffic across the dock and in the immediate vicinity. The official employee exit ideally should be at the opposite end of the hospital so that the chance for exiting employees to come in contact with supplies and equipment in the process of being received is sharply curtailed.

Externally, it is most advisable to place the receiving dock in an area that can be fenced off from the nearest approach road. The basic security approach would be to have the gate and fence closed and locked whenever the receiving dock is unattended. Depending on traffic patterns, in some hospitals this may call for a remote control gate, in others a manually operated gate may suffice.

Internally, provision must be made to permit reliable dual accountability for supplies: They should be identified, verified, and perhaps weighed on the dock, and again verified and counted upon arrival in storage. Since space and flow considerations are of paramount importance here, it is senseless to consider these matters *after* the architectural drawings are approved and construction begun.

At the linen dock, it is essential to prevent linen drivers from having access to other areas of the hospital when they pick up or deliver linen. These pickups are often made in the very early morning when the linen dock may not be watched. Therefore, the linen dock must be sealed off from the rest of the hospital through reliable lockup arrangements or approaches to the dock must be restricted by a gate controlled by a hospital employee who would supervise the linen loading and unloading operation. The importance of such measures is underscored by the fact that stolen supplies and equipment are often transported in soiled linen containers.

A separate trash removal dock also should be provided with similar precautions to prevent unsupervised access by drivers during trash loading.

The Employee Exit

Employee pilferage can be curtailed if all employees are required to enter and depart from one exit. In hospitals that consist of one main building and only a few auxiliary buildings this goal is attainable.

Channeling the flow of employee traffic through the designated exit, in spite of the availability of numerous fire exits and visitors' lobbies, can be achieved by placing time clocks and locker rooms in strategic locations. Another consideration is the location of the employee parking lot to permit easy access during inclement weather.

Linen Security

Linen is usually a most vulnerable supply item; it is easily disposed of at a good price, making it a tempting target for pilferage by employees, patients, and visitors. Moreover, linen on the nursing floors is a supply item requiring the most frequent access by nurses and aides. Great care must therefore be taken in the relative location of nursing stations and other patient care areas to the location of linen closets or alcoves where linen carts are to be stored.

Similarly, regional storage rooms have to be subject to specialized protection arrangements. If such areas are in close proximity to heavily trafficked corridors, or can be entered through accessible windows or fire exits, protection by some form of electronic intrusion alarm equipment has to be considered.

If the hospital maintains its own laundry within its

complex, special intrusion protection may have to be designed to protect the laundry during periods when there is no one in attendance.

Storage Areas

Space availability and fire laws permitting, it is advantageous to design areas such as central surgical supply, general storage, or maintenance supply and tools' crib areas in such a way that there is no direct exit through fire doors, nor any connection to the outside through windows. If this is not possible, consideration should be given to some form of electronic intrusion alarm protection; alarms should be placed on all fire doors.

Such arrangements should be taken into consideration when the grand master and sub-master key setups are designed.

Protection of Food

Failure to control the handling and storage of fresh meats and poultry properly can be very costly. It is vital, therefore, for the location of meat freezers and coolers, and storage areas for canned meats and poultry to be carefully selected. These areas must also be provided with suitable lockup devices during the planning phase.

Canned staple foods are second in priority from a security point of view. Reliable lockup hardware as well as possible intrusion protection by electronic means, depending upon the location of the food storage area, have to be considered.

Lockup of dairy and produce freezers and coolers usually does not have to be quite as rigid as the system protecting the meat storage area.

Pharmacy

Lockup requirements for narcotics and hypnotic drugs are clearly stipulated by federal and state laws.

As a general rule it is best to design the central pharmacy or any subsidiary pharmacy which may serve the clinics in such a way as to limit access to pharmacists and their assistants only. This is often accomplished by equipping pharmacies with Dutch-type doors or ledge-equipped windows, through which all negotiations between pharmacists and nursing personnel can take place.

Emergency Room and Outpatient Clinics

The protection of individuals is of paramount importance in emergency rooms and outpatient clinics. Many clinics cannot safely function without guard coverage. A great deal can be done in the design and planning of these clinics to reduce opportunities for physical assault on the staff.

Nurses' Residence

Whether the nurses' residence is part of the complex or is a separate building connected by tunnel or bridge, entrance to the residence should be monitored. Monitoring can be achieved by guard coverage. Good advance planning, however, can sometimes achieve effective monitoring for protection without additional payroll expense for guards. Such devices as closed-circuit TV, surveillance, public address systems, various types of door alarms, and other mechanical or electronic devices can often be used instead.

Perimeter Security

Here there are a wide variety of problems, and many solutions are possible. There is little similarity between a rural or suburban hospital built on a large expanse of land, and an urban hospital consisting of one massive or several adjacent buildings, covering one or more city blocks. But the essential objective for perimeter security remains the same regardless of the site.

The complex should be designed so as to inhibit an employee, visitor, or any person entering the hospital to emerge unobserved and unimpeded through a fire exit or any other door, window, air shaft, or fire escape.

To attain this goal requires a comprehensive lockup system within existing fire regulations, supported by a practical monitor alarm system which deters and also exposes breaches of the perimeter.

The Guard Force

It is rare that a guard post, whether fixed or roving, can be justified on economic grounds unless the guard is required to perform multiple security duties. It is usually difficult to justify a guard's exclusive attention to the monitoring of employee traffic, or the surveillance of patients in the emergency room, or the watching of activities on the receiving dock.

However, if guard duties, coverage, and schedules are formulated during the blueprint stage, plans can incorporate physical and procedural measures permitting guard flexibility which makes their costs more tolerable.

Conclusion

The presentation of these observations, of course, cannot be considered all-inclusive. This overview of administrative controls, physical requirements, and policy considerations that are applicable to hospitals should demonstrate that although the problems are complex, they are manageable through forethought and timing. Architects can make a contribution second to none in this grave and costly area by incorporating security considerations in their plans. Fortunately, some leading professionals are moving in this direction, but the response has been minor compared to the need.

13 CASTLES OR PRISONS?

In the previous chapter we considered the essential role of architects in the security design of hospitals. Fortunately, we usually don't have to spend much of our time in hospitals, but most of us spend about one-third of our adult lives in commercial buildings and a good part of the rest in residential buildings.

Unfortunately, as dishonesty and crime are increasing, we are living defensively, adjusting to the tragedy of fear and intimidation as a way of life. When we arrive at our offices we lock the door, and when we return home at night untouched by violence, we double-lock and bolt our doors and say, "We made it today."

The skyscraper office building in particular, so characteristic as a symbol of American business achievement, is for many reasons peculiarly susceptible to invasion by petty thieves, muggers, deviates, and robbers. Even sophisticated New Yorkers were aghast when they read that some intruders bypassed an armed guard in the lobby of an internationally known building and made their way to an office on the nineteenth floor that contained a 500-pound safe. Aware that part of that floor would be occupied during the night but that the twenty-third floor was deserted, the intruders managed to lug the safe up four flights of stairs (using the eleva-

tor would have betrayed their presence to the guard
below) to an empty office, where they proceeded to
dynamite the safe and make off with its contents.

No matter where it is situated, there are plenty of
reasons why the office building is so vulnerable to crime.
For one thing, the multiple entrances any large building must have—and which are required by fire laws—
make access almost laughably easy. The constant coming and going of messengers, repairmen, cleaning and
maintenance staffs, deliverymen, even customers, add
up to one thing, maximum risk.

The list of robberies, bomb threats, and personal
attacks is a long one and still growing. It is no longer
uncommon for a company to have $10,000 worth of
office equipment lifted, for a woman to be attacked in
a corridor, or for an executive to be robbed in the
washroom. Muggings in elevators, stairwells, or lobbies
happen so frequently that they hardly raise an eyebrow.
Furthermore, almost anyone who wants to can gain access to most executive offices; a secretary leaves her desk
for a moment, and when she returns, the purse she left
at her desk is gone.

Even expensive measures are no guarantee. One company installed a host of electronic devices geared to
signal any intrusion during nonworking hours. Nevertheless, electric typewriters, calculators and other expensive equipment continued to disappear every weekend.

Alarmed, the management consulted us. We found a
little bathroom window that could be opened without
setting off any alarms. It was off to one end of the
building, far from most of the operations inside; but
it was only ten feet from the head janitor's closet, and
the intruder obviously knew how to remove the hinge
from the door without even touching the new lock. In
the closet, of course, were the janitor's keys to every

office in the building. So there goes a million-dollar investment in closed circuit TV and all the rest—right out that little bathroom window.

It is not unusual for tenants of office buildings to enter into ten- to twenty-year leases with agents and landlords. The rental may total millions of dollars over the life of the lease. Nor is it uncommon for apartments in co-ops or condominiums to cost anywhere from $50,000 to over $500,000. Substantial sums are spent for interior design, decorators, and legal fees, but how many owners and tenants consider all the aspects of protecting their life and property and that of their employees and guests?

In most cases, the builders, landlords, and agents act as if they are doing tenants a favor by giving any serious consideration to their protection. Firemen visit structures to determine if fire regulations are obeyed, but who checks the premises to make certain that the physical protection of the tenants has been properly provided for? In most cases they are dependent on a doorman, or a superintendent or a guard who may not be physically able to protect himself, let alone have any training on security matters.

No need to tell apartment dwellers that there is a tremendous security problem in too many of the apartment buildings in this nation. Even the finest buildings, in so-called exclusive neighborhoods, have experienced burglaries, muggings, murders, and rapes committed by outsiders.

Now landlords may face legal action if they fail to be concerned and take proper preventive action. A prominent lawyer in New York, Harry H. Lipsig, a specialist in negligence cases, is opening up an entirely new area of negligence. Mr. and Mrs. G. Howard Hodge, residents of a giant "upper-middle-income" apartment complex near Manhattan's famous Lincoln Center, returned home one evening to find two intruders inside their apartment. In the ensuing scuffle, the husband, a music arranger, was struck a fatal blow on the head. His wife, a singer, was beaten. She has retained Lipsig to represent her in a $10-million civil suit against the landlords. If she wins her case, which may take years to litigate, landlords all over the nation will be forced to take far more stringent measures to tighten the security of the buildings they own or manage.

The lesson is clear. If tenants do not insist on adequate protection of life and limb, we shall continue to live and work in fear indefinitely. With the stakes so high, planning for security cannot be developed piece-meal by well-meaning amateurs. The assistance of competent professionals in developing the necessary structural staffing and equipment requirements commands top priority.

14 SECURITY YOU CAN AFFORD

To obtain an objective viewpoint, one individual at a fairly high level should be given the responsibility of evaluating security problems, risks, and countermeasures dispassionately and objectively. He should have access to top management to coordinate and execute approved plans. But most companies do not have such an individual. This is where a professional comes in. He brings to the task of evaluation and recommendation a breadth of experience and an unclouded eye. He can make recommendations from a platform of objectivity. Of course the consultant has something to sell; but his success rests upon results. A reputable consultant will not risk his reputation by loading up a client with measures he does not need, that are too expensive, and that are not likely to work.

There are certain principles that the businessman can apply in deciding whether or not a particular plan is practical. First, he must ask himself if the cost and effort involved are proportionate to the problem. Some protective measures cost more than any conceivable loss they are designed to prevent. It is also possible to err on the other side. For example, a steady trickle of pilferage or shoplifting may be endured because the specific items that are stolen seem trivial in value; this apparent triviality can be deceiving, particularly in businesses that operate on small profit margins. The president of a supermarket chain remarked: "It literally requires $20 in sales to replace one stolen banana. That's an expensive banana."

Then the businessman must ask, is the measure enforceable? Any program that is undertaken should be enforceable with a reasonable and economically feasible security effort. No policy should ever be promulgated unless management is equipped to follow through fully on its execution. Rules that are not fully enforced are worse than no rules at all. They do not deter crime; they encourage dishonest employees by leaving it open to question whether there are any teeth in a particular regulation.

Let's begin with the most common of industrial problems, fraudulent diversion of assets.

There are two principal categories of diversion. One is individual pilferage by employees, visitors, contractors, or intruders. More serious is large-scale theft committed through collusive efforts—collusion between drivers, receivers, shippers, material handlers, maintenance men, janitors; or collusion on the white-collar level, between purchasing agents, vendors, bookkeepers, data processing personnel and the like. An effective security program must be based on realistic assessment of the relative risks and potential losses in both categories of diversion.

First we will take a look at the principle of integrated security that offers maximum possible safeguards against loss in each of the two categories of diversion. Then we'll discuss a method of "honesty insurance" that can provide a broad measure of protection, but which is often overlooked by businessmen as a practical security measure.

INTEGRATED SECURITY

No security program will be effective that is limited to physical protection measures such as lockup devices, alarm systems, surveillance equipment, anti-intrusion devices, or guard coverage. These are essential features, some of which may have to be employed as part of a total security program; however, some of the most far-reaching security problems are procedural in nature.

Since the areas most vulnerable to large-scale diversion are the docks, receiving and loading docks call for the highest combined protection by procedural controls and physical security measures. Though there is no standard formula, a few basic principles can be cited.

Physical separation of receiving from shipping often is essential so that unloading and verification can proceed undisturbed by the loading operation of the outgoing product. By the same token, where raw materials or finished products are highly vulnerable, the loading dock should be separated from the receiving area to preclude any switch of finished goods onto delivery trucks just before they pull out. The mixture of incoming and outgoing loads always poses a security risk.

The dock should be so located so as to keep pedestrian traffic away from the immediate vicinity. Ideally, the official employee exit should be at the opposite side of the plant so that employees entering and leaving have no contact with materials in the process of being received or loaded.

How can employees be forced to use the designated employee exits and prevented from surreptitiously using other available openings such as loading docks and fire exits? The best enforcement technique is to place time clocks and locker rooms in strategic locations, making it difficult for employees to punch out and change their clothes without using the designated exit. Another enforcement tool is the strategic placing of employee parking lots within easy reach of the employee exit. While there should always be a fence separating the plant and the employee parking lot, the parking lot's pedestrian exit should be close enough to the employee entrance to make it easy for employees to reach their cars.

The access of truck drivers to dock areas will of course depend upon loading and unloading practices. There should be continual surveillance, by supervisory personnel or electronic equipment, of the entire loading and unloading process. A suitable drivers' lounge, equipped with minimum facilities so as to limit the presence of drivers in the dock, is another vital security feature.

Should a dock area be separated from the rest of the plant by walls or fencing? If so, what type of gate arrangements will accommodate traffic to and from the dock area? The principal criteria involve the vulnerability and maneuverability of the products being handled. The method of material movement between dock and plant, whether forklift, hand truck, towline, or tow motor train, will be a major deciding factor in the design of fencing and gates.

In many security programs one of the most challenging assignments is to devise an uninterrupted high productivity flow of materials to and from the docks, while providing rigidly controlled checkpoints at the gates. It is here that the strong interplay between physical security measures and procedural controls is most critical.

The trash vehicle is one of the most notorious devices for concealing stolen materials for eventual removal.

Separation of trash accumulation areas and the trash-loading dock, away from both shipping and receiving dock areas, is usually an excellent measure. This is true regardless of whether trash is removed by truck, by exchange of containers, or by compression devices.

One of the key decisions in the security program is whether the approach to the dock areas should be fenced in. If so, decisions have to be made on the type of gates, whether manual or remote controlled, the type of guard coverage at the gates, the question of communication systems between drivers and dock staff. In making these decisions, planners must balance vulnerability against practicality. The type of product received and shipped, the density of truck traffic, and the staffing patterns on the docks are the criteria to consider. In urban locations, where fencing is physically impossible, the combined physical security and procedural control system assumes paramount importance. On rural sites the arguments may weigh in favor of fencing. In such cases, guard coverage at the gate usually can provide some meaningful monitoring functions.

In developing a comprehensive security program for any plant, it is essential to chart the anticipated traffic patterns, including both vehicular and pedestrian traffic. The control measures directed at truck traffic will of course be directly connected with the security program covering the receiving and loading docks. Visitor traffic should be channeled according to strictly defined rules. Employee traffic can be best controlled by funneling all employees entering and leaving the plant through an exit exclusively serving employee traffic. In large plants it is unacceptable to funnel employee traffic through openings that also serve other traffic.

Particular attention should be given to traffic involving contractors and their employees. Virtually every industrial plant accommodates some traffic by outside contractors, if only the various service companies operating food, beverage, and cigarette vending machines. If an industrial plant makes constant use of outside building contractors, a separate set of regulations has to cover the control over their vehicles, equipment, and personnel. In many plants a serious security loophole is tolerated as a result of the necessity for contractors to bring in equipment and supplies in their own trucks and station wagons. This opens dangerous possibilities for large-scale diversion of goods disguised as contractor-owned supplies or equipment.

Where a plant consists of one compact building, traffic control is often easily achieved. Where a plant consists of numerous buildings sprawling over a large site, it is more difficult to accomplish.

Internal protection involves a system of selective inaccessibility. Whether specific equipment or materials require caging or storage in lockable rooms or enclosures depends upon a combination of factors: value, disposability at a profit, as well as susceptibility to damage by sabotage. Therefore there is no standardized solution; each plant's selective internal security arrangement must be individually tailored.

The internal lockup systems must dovetail with the shift pattern under which the plant operates. If part of a plant runs three shifts, a decision as to whether the idle sections of the plant have to be tightly secured from intrusion depends upon the vulnerability of equipment and materials. It is often wise to design lockup facilities in such a way that the lockup patterns can be revised as the shift patterns change.

An integral part of the security program is a clearly defined set of regulations governing the issuance of individual keys, master keys, and grand masters. The system has to include a method of authorization for key issuance, and an easily enforceable retrieval procedure.

In designing the alarm system, planners face a wide variety of choices. There are no two plants anywhere in the United States that require the same alarm system, no matter how similar they are in design. There are some plants where any capital budget or maintenance expenditure for an alarm system would be a total waste—plants in rural areas protected by total fencing and experiencing a type of vehicular and pedestrian traffic that is easily controlled through other means. There are other plants which require the most sophisticated burglary alarm systems protecting the entire perimeter, supported by strategically located internal intrusion alarms of the microwave or ultrasonic or photoelectric cell variety. Some such plants are insufficiently protected if the intrusion alarms are limited to the street perimeter. Some plants require alarm protection of upper floors; some require sophisticated intrusion detectors along the roof lines.

In some plants electronic intrusion detectors placed internally and trained on specific selected areas may be the most vital alarm installations; in fact, there are plants where internal alarming of selected areas is the only alarm installation that is economically justified. One crucial decision is the monitoring method. There is a wide choice in this area, ranging from central monitoring stations permanently manned and operated by plant security personnel exclusively, to central monitoring stations operated by local security agencies or by telephone answering services. Some plants are best served by a compromise arrangement using part of various alternatives.

Guards must never constitute the exclusive security measure in any one area. The guard force can be a valuable supporting agent, however, in many specific areas, including materials movement, dock security, and traffic control.

One of the greatest challenges in designing a total security program is incorporating guard coverage which is effective and economically justifiable. A guard who has but one post and one target to observe—be it a parking lot or a specific gate—is in most cases an unprofitable investment. The guard should have a variety of responsibilities. This not only makes him more economically feasible; it keeps him alert. A bored guard is going to be just as ineffective as a guard who is unreasonably overloaded with work.

HONESTY INSURANCE

The fidelity bond is an economical and much neglected means of protection. But it is even more: The mere use of the bonding form can be a most effective screening device. The screening takes place without fuss or embarrassment. We see it happening when a job applicant who has just found out that bonding is a requirement makes some excuse to leave the room and does not come back.

There is an amazing ignorance among businessmen regarding bonding. They think of it as some special procedure that is applied only in cases of the most extreme risk. They consider it expensive. They feel that it is demeaning in that it imputes potential dishonesty to the person who is bonded.

Bonding is none of these things. It is not expensive. It is a common-sense procedure to apply to anyone who will be employed in any responsible position. The employer can say, and mean, that bonding is a *privilege* —that it is a specific and tangible bestowal of trust upon the person who is going to work for the company.

Even when a company does use bonding, it may not

use it properly. In many instances, we have found that neither the employer nor employees are aware that the company carries this honesty insurance. As a result, the company fails to reap the vital psychological benefits from bonding. Thus management forfeits a valuable deterrent. Employees should be informed that they are bonded, and should understand both the privileges and the penalties.

Any insurance specialist can spell out all the details of bonding.

Insurance policies provide coverage for losses occurring under specified conditions. Policies also require that in the event of a loss, notice must be given to the carrier without undue delay, and proof of loss submitted by the insured, in accordance with the terms of the policy. The insured is usually given ninety days after discovery of a loss in which to file a proof of loss with the carrier. Carriers usually will grant a reasonable extension, if it's required. "Proof of loss" means literally presenting the facts that establish beyond a reasonable doubt that you have sustained a loss.

A proof of loss is usually prepared by the top financial executive, in collaboration with the corporate insurance department if the company has one. It is also advisable that the opinion of the company's legal advisor be sought in the preparation of the claim. However, many companies do not have available staff to handle this technical procedure, and it is therefore imperative that outside experts be engaged.

You cannot expect your broker to assemble the information required in an involved loss. But your broker should have a strong rapport with the carriers, and should assume a large share of responsibility in getting your claim off the ground in its preliminary stage. In some cases, claims can be quickly and amicably settled by your broker; then the proof of loss becomes a formality.

Although book losses are dollar losses, as a rule they are not covered unless it can be established beyond a reasonable doubt that the shortage is due to theft or manipulation. It is always incumbent on the policyholder to prove his claim. The type of proof required varies with the type of coverage specified in the policy.

It is surprising that many knowledgeable people in business today are not aware of what is basic in the filing of a claim. Many labor under the delusion that if they have a loss, all they have to do is to notify the insurance company, and the insurance company will develop the claim and pay. The fact is that the function of the insurance company is to pay the loss provided it is presented with all the facts involved, and provided the facts fall within the requirements of the policy. So the burden of proof falls on the policyholder. Problems are always created when claims are not properly prepared and substantiated, and this nearly always happens because of inexperience and improper guidance in the development of the claim and the preparation of the proof of loss.

It is not always advantageous to have an individual from your own organization attempt to determine the full amount of the loss or the identity of all the persons involved, because he may unknowingly alert the culprits without obtaining results, or may even be involved himself. Consequently you could prejudice your claim with the bonding company and may ultimately end up unjustly blaming your insurance broker or your carrier for your own failure.

The skilled fact-finder, if he has some indication of the facts concerning the loss, can blueprint the steps necessary to reconstruct the extent of the loss as well as pertinent past events. Uncovering the extent of the theft and identifying the persons involved, at all occupational levels, requires unusual skill in interviewing and sophisticated knowledge of behavioral science.

The statement of the person interviewed should be as detailed as possible, including names and addresses of persons implicated, dates, quantity or dollar amounts, how the thefts were accomplished, and the disposition of the stolen assets. It should also contain information about the person's mode of living: outstanding debts, mortgages, loans, previous marriages, child support, and other obligations, and personal weaknesses such as gambling, drinking, or drug abuse.

There is another, little-known angle you should be cautious about. Suppose you have sustained a loss through employee theft which the employee has a legal obligation to make good, and which is also covered under your blanket bond. You may feel that you are strengthening your case by accepting a promissory note from the culprit; however, in fact, you may be depriving yourself of the insurance that your policy provides. If there is to be any form of restitution accepted, it is best to have it handled by your legal counsel. When you accept such a promissory note you have resolved the employee's obligation to repay; the obligation may become simply a debt which will be your obligation to collect—and you may be releasing the insurance company of its obligation to pay. This is most likely to happen when you are overzealous but not sufficiently knowledgeable.

Almost all blanket bonds contain a clause which automatically excludes an employee from coverage after the employer learns of a dishonest act on the employee's part. If an employee is involved in dishonesty, yet remains on your payroll, you are waiving your rights with the insurance company. If subsequently he becomes involved in any form of dishonesty, he is excluded from coverage, unless you have obtained from your carrier an express waiver of the risk.

In a recent case an employee acknowledged that he had stolen in excess of $150,000 worth of precious metal from the company. His personnel file revealed that the man was involved in the theft of some tools and other equipment three years earlier; he had been reprimanded and put back to work. Despite the fact that the man was arrested and convicted of the second theft, the claim was denied by the insurance company because there was prior knowledge of involvement.

Also, if you learn that one of your employees has committed a crime even some years prior to your employing him, you should determine whether this circumstance excludes him from your bond.

The federal government has for some years sponsored a program, administered through state employment offices, which facilitates the hiring or the retention of persons not eligible for bonding under the employer's policy. If these persons prove that they need a bond in order to obtain or to hold a job, the government will furnish a bond up to $10,000, depending on the risk, without cost to the employee or employer.

The ultimate responsibility for security should be a high-level executive who should function as overall security coordinator. Part of his duties will be to resolve conflicting goals and competing interests—to balance on the one hand physical security requirements and accountability controls, and on the other hand the needs for operational efficiency standards, acceptable cost structures, and enforceable employee regulations.

Preventive management is the best deterrent to business dishonesty. As outlined in this book, it goes beyond the area of security. It lies at the heart of a well-run and profitable business or institution.

SUMMARY—QUESTIONS AND ANSWERS

The best summary of our experience that we can offer is in the form of answers to the questions we are most frequently asked by executives.

Q. *How much is employee crime costing business in the United States and Canada?*

A. Employees steal more than $15 million a day in cash and merchandise—about $5 billion a year. When you add kickbacks, theft of company secrets, and other malpractices, the total is probably several times greater than that. Kickback payments, alone, we estimate, amount to $5 billion a year. The only groups who claim that kickbacks are on the decline are the purchasing agents' associations.

Q. *What does this mean to the average consumer?*

A. It means that 15 percent of the price you and I pay for goods and services goes to cover the cost of dishonesty.

Q. *Is this sort of crime on the rise?*

A. Yes. Crime and vandalism in the street are being overshadowed by crime in business. Employee dishonesty has reached an all-time high, and threatens to double in the next five years if recent trends prevail. Right now, there is more than a 50 percent chance of substantial dishonesty in any firm, and a 75 percent chance of harmful malpractice.

Q. *Who is doing the stealing?*

A. People at all levels. No "typical" thief exists. Our

statistics, based on more than 200 clients listed on the stock exchange and many others in diversified fields, show that the greatest amount of dishonesty, dollarwise, occurs among supervisory employees and executives.

Similarly, there is no "typical" embezzler. An aura of respectability is probably the most common denominator. Curiously, the malpractices that receive the least attention are those committed by "trusted" employees whose opportunities are great, whose methods are less subject to scrutiny—and who are last to be suspected.

Nor are women immune to crime. They are just as adept as men at stealing from their employers. More and more women hold positions of trust in the work force today, as buyers, bookkeepers, cashiers, and executives. In retail stores, for example, females have greater exposure to money and merchandise and are consequently responsible for more wrongdoings than their male co-workers.

We find that females become dishonest for a number of reasons, some of them quite different from the forces that lure men into dishonesty. Primarily men are interested in money per se, whereas women are covetous of what money will buy, and they will fight harder to keep up an expensive front than will men. Moreover, a woman very often feels insecure because of family responsibilities and fears of losing job, and she steals to build up a bulwark against the possibility.

Q. *What is the practical approach to uncovering theft?*

A. Practical exposure of theft is best initiated by a thorough, ear-to-the-ground examination of the company's operations. When kickbacks, theft of company secrets and assets, destruction of records, manipulations, or embezzlement are suspected, a specialist is needed to develop a program that will:

> Uncover and develop the full extent of the loss. Substantiate the loss with incontroverti-

ble facts. Recover the maximum to which you
are justly entitled under your fidelity bond.
Establish preventive controls that are easy
to enforce and that will protect the company's
assets.

Uncovering the extent of the theft and the persons
involved requires unusual skills in interviewing and in
the application of behavioral sciences. Documenting
your losses without robbing a person of his dignity is of
paramount importance—first, out of human decency and
second, because the suspect may actually be innocent.

Q. *What* are *the underlying conditions of white collar
crime?*

A. Failure to establish enforceable controls and procedures. Rapid growth and prosperity bring about permissiveness and neglect by top management. Dishonesty
is a by-product of poor management. It isn't lack of
morality; we are all basically good people. The problem
starts with inattention by top executives. A middle-
management man once told me, "I knew that some of
my employees were stealing, but I had no real choice.
I had to go along to protect my job."

If an executive sits back and says, "I told my people
to be honest; therefore, it is not my responsibility," he is
shirking his duty. A corporate official lives in a fish bowl.
He is susceptible to criticism from the public and to law-
suits from the stockholders. Recent court decisions have
held executives and directors, as well as public accounting firms, responsible for failure to aggressively pursue
evidence of dishonesty.

Q. *What makes honest people dishonest?*

A. First, there has to be opportunity. And management must accept responsibility for this element, since
it usually stems from poor supervision or bad examples
set by others. Sometimes the principals of companies
create their own dilemma by using double standards.
Nothing breaks down discipline so rapidly or lessens

respect for management and controls. Policies must be applicable to all levels.

Second, an employee often steals to get over a difficult period. Slowly, it becomes a built-in habit. Then the rationale comes very easily. The employee performs the act and justifies his behavior. He tells himself: "My boss doesn't appreciate my work; the other fellow is getting more money than I am. The company owes it to me. Everyone is stealing, why not me?"

The most common characteristic of these people is an appearance of sincerity that lulls management into trusting them. We are all basically insecure—under given pressures we are bound to bend.

Q. *Are all acts of dishonesty or malpractice for personal gain?*

A. No. Many losses are sustained because of frustration and spite. I recall a shipping clerk who had been with a distributor for eleven years. Everyone in the company loved him. Nothing was too much for him. Suddenly, the company was bought out by a mail-order house. The mail-order house promoted him to head of its order-picking department, but did not give him the equipment or people necessary to do the job. They just gave him more and more work. Instead of appreciating him, they yelled at him. He said this in his statement: "Sometimes the boss gave me bills and orders to match up, and I was unable to match them, with all my other duties. So, I tore them up—about 300 new orders a week—and finished on time and my boss said, 'Thank you!'"

Q. *Do many executives who steal get arrested?*

A. I don't know how many are caught, but we do know that many corporations are reluctant to turn in their employees. Primarily, they don't want the bad publicity. Second, it is a drawn-out procedure, and they don't feel it is worth the effort.

It would appear that government at all levels provides

virtually no deterrent to business crime because, based on recent statistics, less than 5 percent of the offenders end up before the courts, and approximately 1 percent are sent to jail.

Bascially, the people involved in embezzlement, fraud, kickbacks, and stealing company secrets are not the criminal type. Many get suspended sentences. So what's the upshot? An arrest is important if it serves a purpose. A crime has been committed; yes, the people responsible should pay the price—I am a strong believer in that—but it is also important to be practical and seek to recover lost assets. Lie detector tests may implicate a man, but as a rule, this does not fortify your claim with the necessary backup to prove to your insurance carrier the full extent of your loss.

Q. *What effect do mergers and acquisitions have on the problem?*

A. The recurrent wave of corporate mergers and acquisitions is having a marked influence on business crime that extends heavily into the executive suite. Mergers, instead of making a contribution to corporate profits, can create a drain. Sometimes they foster disloyalty due to insecurity and unfulfilled expectations, as detailed in that amusing book, *Welcome to Our Conglomerate, You're Fired.*

Q. *How do kickbacks hurt a business?*

A. The margin of profit between a manufacturer's cost and selling price, in most lines of business, is not wide enough to support any kickback payments designed to generate business. On the other side, when gratuities are the standard, the customer firm is generally accepting a product of lesser quality or a short count, or is paying a higher price.

Q. *How are kickbacks concealed?*

A. Kickbacks are very sophisticated today. Although some people do accept cash, there are more subtle ways of taking kickbacks—unsecured loans, use of credit cards, and so on. They set up dummy corporations under their wives' maiden names; they get a percentage of the business; they become highly paid consultants.

Q. *Are inventory shortages a major problem?*

A. Yes, indeed. Many corporate financial statements show reduction in profits, or outright losses, despite increased sales largely because of inventory shortages. According to the latest available figures for conventional department stores, inventory "shrinkage"—a trade euphemism for unexplained losses—is between 2 and 3 percent for each dollar of sales. Discount stores' inventory losses are as high as 5 percent of sales.

Q. *Is this the result of employee theft?*

A. The bulk of it is. One of our recent studies shows that 70 percent of all inventory losses are due to employee theft.

Q. *And the other 30 percent?*

A. Although shoplifting makes the headlines, as a rule it accounts for only 15 percent; bookkeeping errors and manipulations make up the rest.

Q. *What is the reaction of businessmen to this?*

A. As profits decrease, many executives panic and out of fear, resort to running their business as an armed camp, utilizing lie detector tests, closed-circuit TV, and guard saturation.

This is the wrong philosophy, and it does not work. In many cases, it has been counterproductive in terms of solving the problem and has adversely affected employee morale. Furthermore, at the retail level it has frightened away the buying public and inhibited their normal shopping habits.

Q. *You mentioned manipulation. What do you mean by that?*

A. The fact that company books show increased sales does not necessarily mean that profits are greater. We have seen too many instances of employees manipulating records to cover up defalcations or to simulate achievement of unrealistic goals. The net effect is that the company unwittingly pays taxes on nonexistent profits.

Another type of manipulation: How many poor scrap dealers do you know? It could be your own employees helped to make one rich. Brass and copper, for instance, are sometimes deliberately mixed together and go out as scrap for a pittance of their value.

Q. *Do some types of business have more problems with internal crime than others?*

A. With theft constituting a multi-billion dollar drain on industry profits, probably no business is immune. Business crime today has become a well-paying, low-risk, tax-free enterprise. There is scarcely any business that is not affected by it.

Some businesses are obviously more vulnerable:
• Retailing, for example, because of the size of many operations.
• The construction industry, where opportunity for dishonesty pervades every aspect and takes many forms including falsification of accounting records; padding of payroll; theft of tools, supplies, and equipment; kickbacks; sabotage; substitution of substandard items; conflicts of interest including revelation of bids to competitors, conspiracy on bids, prearranged change orders, etc.
• The wholesale-distribution industry is experiencing serious problems, and is particularly vulnerable because the same dollar loss has a greater impact on profits, due to its traditionally lower markup; its method of accounting, which masks the full extent of inventory losses; its promotional efforts, including free goods, trade-ins, and return privileges; and collusion between employees of wholesalers and their customers.
• The service industries—for example, hotels and hos-

pitals—in which operations are not only big business but a complex of many businesses. Employee dishonesty, waste, and indifference are prime factors in increased costs. Theft of supplies, equipment, food, drugs, and narcotics by hospital employees has reached heights which are dangerous under any circumstances, but intolerable in institutions concerned with health.

It is too easy to attribute these escalating losses to decline in moral standards. In many organizations, pervasive slackening of what was once a tightly run ship has trickled through to the ranks.

Q. *What can be done to control internal business crime?*

A. In more than forty years of helping management control losses and strengthen systems, we have concluded that stealing is as contagious as the measles. Fortunately, it is also as curable, provided the proper dosage of preventive management is administered.

Top management must accept the fact that supervisory and departmental failings exist in their company, and must assume the responsibility for concern and direction in the effort to uncover the hard facts about dishonesty. If they are not finding it, they are probably not looking for it.

Executives must develop a total approach toward preventing malpractices within their organizations. Experience has shown that the first step should be an "Inventory of Exposure." This is a comprehensive security program engineered to protect the assets, both tangible and intangible, of the business. Excellence and control in one area can be nullified by neglect in others.

Preventive management equals good business practices. By adequately protecting its assets, management can not only reduce losses through dishonesty, but can also preserve important moral values.